AFTER THE PANDEMIC
VISIONS OF LIFE POST COVID-19

LAWRENCE KNORR

BARBARA MATTHEWS

CHRIS FENWICK

CHERYL WOODRUFF-BROOKS

PAT LAMARCHE

WILL DELAVAN

SCOTT ZUCKERMAN

MERRILL SHAFFER

MARIANNE BICKETT

VIRGINIA BRACKETT

H. A. CALLUM

TORY GATES

CATHERINE JORDAN

WYLIE MCLALLEN

MARK CARLSON

THOMAS MALAFARINA

MAIA WILLIAMSON

PENNY FLETCHER

IRIS DORBIAN

BROOK LENKER

JACK ADLER

JOSEPH MAZERAC

BRIDGET SMITH

SIMON LANDRY

WYNNE KINDER

SUNBURY PRESS

Mechanicsburg, PA USA

Published by Sunbury Press, Inc.
Mechanicsburg, Pennsylvania

SUNBURY
P R E S S

www.sunburypress.com

For information about special discounts for bulk purchases, please contact Sunbury Press Orders Dept. at (855) 338-8359 or orders@sunburypress.com.

To request one of our authors for speaking engagements or book signings, please contact Sunbury Press Publicity Dept. at publicity@sunburypress.com.

FIRST SUNBURY PRESS EDITION: May 2020

Set in Adobe Garamond | Interior design by Crystal Devine | Cover design by Lawrence Knorr | Edited by Lawrence Knorr.

Publisher's Cataloging-in-Publication Data
Names: Knorr, Lawrence, editor, author | et al, authors.
Title: After the pandemic : visions after life post COVID-19 / Lawrence Knorr, et al.
Description: First trade paperback edition. | Mechanicsburg, PA : Sunbury Press, 2020.
Summary: Sunbury Press authors envision how the world will be after the COVID-19 pandemic abates.
Identifiers: ISBN: 978-1-620067-00-0 (softcover).
Subjects: SOCIAL SCIENCE / Disease & Health Issues | SOCIAL SCIENCE / Essays | BUSINESS & ECONOMICS / Economic Conditions.

Product of the United States of America
0 1 1 2 3 5 8 13 21 34 55

Continue the Enlightenment!

CONTENTS

INTRODUCTION

AT SUNBURY PRESS, I recently reported to our hundreds of authors that we were off to our best start ever, but all of this seems trivial given what we are facing. Now is not the time for celebrating sales projections, nor is it the time for fearmongering. Instead, it is the time for rational thought, which is the whole premise behind our company slogan: Continue the Enlightenment.

The Enlightenment was a time when our Western society began seeking answers outside of just our religion. Here in the 21st century, it is clear, as humans, we still have extraordinarily little control of our world, nor do we have solutions to our most significant problems. Thus, Enlightenment in the 21st century is a merging of science, religion, philosophy, and other disciplines in search of the truth.

To be clear, I am not just talking about technology. Nikola Tesla once said: "There is a difference between progress and technology, progress benefits humanity. Technology does not necessarily do that." Despite all our progress and technology over recent centuries, we are still susceptible to the tiniest of things—a virus. In fact, because of our technology, we might be even more vulnerable. Permit me to explain.

Some of you know I have had a long career in information technology, from a programmer to a CIO. I have been responsible for all information technology for a multi-billion-dollar retailer. I am not saying this to brag. I am saying this as a confession—despite this, I have no answers to our global problems. I helped to push us closer to a precarious edge. Those of you who have visited a grocery store in recent days know exactly what I am talking about. Our technology has helped us be more efficient in the distribution of goods—so much so that we now make nearly everything just-in-time and stock only what the system tells us we need. For decades we have worked to make our supply chains more streamlined and to connect the world in the most cost-effective trade network. Now, when we need it most, we are finding empty shelves. Now, when we need it most, a lot of our production is overseas. Technology—yes. Progress—no!

Reflecting on this, I spent some time in my library the other day looking for a book I had forgotten about and tucked away. Joseph Tainter, back in the 1980s, wrote a classic on this topic called *The Collapse of Complex Societies*. Dr. Tainter researched the many great civilizations of the past that are now nothing more than toppled monuments. Countless hours of documentaries and speculative programming have covered the mysterious collapse of these societies. At the root of Tainter's thesis is the premise that societies evolve to exceed their basic survival capacity. In other words, they unwittingly advance beyond a sustainable point and become vulnerable to collapse. At that time, this was a ground-breaking work on archaeology. Then, over the years, many began to see it as a blueprint for what might happen to us.

To summarize Tainter differently, the Great Pyramid is not just an enigmatic wonder of the world. It is also a stark reminder that societies rise and fall. Knowledge is gained and forgotten. In many ways, we have progressed technologically, but we have yet to achieve the ability to recreate something wondrous built thousands of years ago.

Turning back to Enlightenment, once again, Mother Nature is reminding us, we are not in control. If you are a religious person, you might be thinking God is teaching us another lesson about humility. If you are scientific-minded, you might be reminded that what we know about our universe is but a speck compared to what could be known. A more philosophical person might seek a rational explanation of how to cope with our human experience. Just know we are all right in our own way. Everyone has a contribution to make in this debate. These are times to take care of one another and to cooperate. We need to set aside our differences and work together towards real progress. The survival of our society depends on it.

This volume contains twenty-seven chapters written by twenty-five different authors who focused on their visions for the post-COVID-19 world. These are honest, heartfelt observations tapping their expertise, from medicine to economics, to the arts, to sports, to philosophy, and many other subjects. Most of these vision statements are hopeful and optimistic, but they all agree on one thing. The world is changing due to the impacts of the pandemic.

Thank you for opening this book. We all hope you enjoy the content you are about to read. Please stay healthy and remember our company slogan to "Continue the Enlightenment."

Lawrence Knorr
April 27, 2020

CHANGE AND EMBRACING IT

BY TORY GATES

I HAVE BEEN watching the coronavirus pandemic, and all that has gone with it from a unique angle. I am watching the world continue to turn around me, and with that, the one question that I keep asking myself is, "Are we finally going to change?"

Something must, and I have long believed it is us.

We, as a first-world nation (like that means something), must finally accept that the lives we have known and lived, and those of our preceding generations, are going to change. Not end, but they will be altered.

Humanity has primarily built itself a little kingdom by the sea, with many smaller ones that we tend to ignore. We are good at ignoring things; endless wars, some of which our nation started or was involved in, the suffering and carnage that comes from those. Our environment is slowly decaying, yet we don't listen; too many of us claim it's not happening, or as one caller to a talk show I produced proclaimed, "I'm going to be dead by then anyway, so who cares?"

There you have it. Arrogance, self-centeredness, privilege, and with that comes lashing out against anyone or anything that dares to say otherwise. All of this has one central, emotional element.

FEAR

We are terrified of anything we do not understand or refuse to understand. Certainly, not all of us feel this way. The problems our world faces are serious, and the quicker we act, the better all will be, along with the future generations many talk a lot about, but do not seem to care about all that much.

The pandemic is only starting here, and I am afraid it is going to get much worse before it gets better. A friend who lives in Italy says a nation in lockdown is terrifying; she does not leave her apartment, but her mother does on occasion. A once vibrant country has gone silent.

Other countries are doing the same things: stay in place orders, closing off public spaces, only essential services may open. Think of that on a national scale and think of it where you are.

I work in an industry that deems us essential personnel, in broadcasting. Yes, I am a member of that boogeyman you like to slag, "The Media." From behind your keyboards, you cut and paste and pound out the constant mantra that we are making this up, lying to you, out to get the president, *ad nauseum*.

I am here to tell you that I am not one of those well paid, well known, puffed up peacocks, who are only telling you what they are told to regurgitate. I have spent more than thirty-five years in this business; I have been a deejay, a producer, a journalist, a traffic reporter, a talk-show host, a manager of stations, pretty much all of it.

I work for a statewide news network, I work for an AM/FM combo in the Lebanon Valley, and I work for a big conglomerate of stations as well. I am a jobber, but it is what I do. Never in my career have I put out stories that I knew not to be true, to the best of the ability of myself and those around me. We do not deal in bullshit. We do the best we can to give you what we know to be accurate, like it or not. You do not have to like it.

That leads me to the experience you and I are having right now. You would think I am outgoing and all that; behind a microphone, I can be, but I must be, to talk to you. I am generally not; I prefer my own company, and I often say I prefer the company of my cats to people.

This weekend, I will spend a second three-day period at home, not because of my health, but because I have no place I need to go. It is interesting, isn't it? We build a home or rent one, and we take pride in it, but the first chance we get, we go out.

And where do we go? You fill in the blank but look now at what is closed. Ballparks, stadiums, concert venues, restaurants, coffee shops (my personal favorite), and even some open spaces are now shut down. We are suddenly not what we were, as those things defined us.

I honestly hope we have not had to retrain ourselves how to wash our hands. The fascination with germs and keeping them away, I think, assisted us a little.

The Chinese did one good thing in their message to the people, practice the basics, wash your hands, and keep yourself and your spaces clean. That, more than anything, will make a difference.

Meanwhile, as science struggles to find a vaccine, a cure, something, we must do our part, and that means in large part, rousing ourselves from our previous lives, and rethinking what we are going to do.

Fear is a real emotion, and all living beings feel it. We do not like to admit it, but it is there. You see it in the panic buying, with store shelves being emptied as if we are headed for a nuclear war or a dystopian nightmare. Funny, we love reading those types of stories and watching them on TV, but we sure do not want to live them, do we?

Much does not have to change. Not saying I am doing it right, but as a person who prefers to be alone, I shop when I need, not because fear has crazed me. My neighbors are looking out for each other. There is a strong sense that we will get through this, as we did all other things, worse things.

But again, we must embrace change. Modern technology has done some good things; we can communicate faster, more efficiently. Working from home is like a dream to a lot of folks; you still need a human presence; that element will never go away.

More and more, though, we see the benefits of that. You do not have to drive hours a day through traffic to get to an office that much anymore when you can stay home. You can see your family a bit more (if that is what you want), and at times it is fun to write with my cat Baldrick in my lap. He also joins me on camera for my online radio program, which I stream on Facebook. He is not the first of my "kids" to do that; my departed Sofia also did, and she became a watched-for sidekick.

The carbon footprint is going to be smaller. How about that? Less greenhouse gases, more use of mass transit, perchance?

Now the way we consume is the big one. Online shopping? I admit I do it as well. The book, music, and other shops are going by the way, but we do lose an element of human contact. That's why you find me in a coffee place or a bookshop a lot because I can smell out more of my kind.

All of this comes back around to another problem we humans have: the past. We live in it. We have nostalgia for the "good old days," the happy times when things seemed so much simpler. That is something we use darkly because older generations rail against the younger. I remember people saying younger folk express themselves too much.

Really? And you are doing what? I guess freedom of speech and expression is only for certain people, huh? We see that in our political, religious, and social rhetoric. We attack, assault and threaten those who make us feel threatened, and for what? It will not do you any good, so think before you press "send" next time.

Here is where I think we are: the good times are all gone, those of a time that is no longer here, and is of no use to us, but for a point of reference. The question becomes, what now do we do?

The pandemic has made us aware of our humanity and our frailty. We always think we are strong enough, tough enough, or are protected in some way that we cannot get sick. It will not happen to us. We will not die.

Well, we all do. Right now, while we shelter, take stock of ourselves, and create as many of us are wont to do, we also have time to think, really think. I do not believe our lifestyle has to change that much, but we must all rethink our way of living. We may not be able to afford as much, do as much, go places as much, and yet we must do this if ever we are to progress as human beings. One word keeps coming to mind.

APPRECIATION

You never do realize you miss a person, be it a loved one, a friend, a pet, or a place until it is no longer there. Juxtapose our situation right now: I have not heard it that much, but there's the grumbling and complaining, we can't watch sports or go to it, we can't go out, we can't do this, that, etc. Some also complain about how unfair this is when they feel all right.

Tell that to those who have died if you can. Or the families of those lost, or who are suffering right now. You would probably get your ass kicked for it.

Am I concerned about myself? Yes, I am. I have health issues, which make me susceptible, but I have a job to do, and I will do it.

I appreciate seeing my fellow artists performing free online concerts. Some are stuck overseas and cannot get home, but they are making the best of it. Music and art of any kind are things that have always brought out the good in us, and we are all finding ourselves busy.

I spent the past weekend hammering out the first draft of a new book. I would say that was a pretty decent use of my free time within the walls. I am sure my fellows are at least thinking about their creations, or what is coming.

I have time to appreciate my two iPods loaded with music, putting them on shuffle and letting them motivate me as I write. There are so many possibilities.

My friend Soji who lives in York has called on fellow musicians (as I occasionally am) to come out and play a show once we get the all-clear. We will get there, and here is my parting shot.

When we can step back into our favorite places, see our friends again, and do in public the things we once took for granted, I know I will appreciate every one of those moments even more. I will be there, breathe it in, and know we are better human beings for what we fought through and survived. Do this. We can do any damn thing we set our minds to.

Peace, out.

〔 ABOUT THE AUTHOR 〕

TORY GATES is a writer of young adult/crossover fiction that takes readers back in time, to exotic locales and deals in social and human issues. His third book for Brown Posey Press, *Searching for Roy Buchanan*, is the first of a YA/time travel series. The sequel, *Call it Love*, is set for release in 2020.

A broadcaster with more than thirty years behind the microphone, Tory hosts The Brown Posey Press Show, a program for authors on the BookSpeak Network. He also presents programs on music and public affairs for radio stations across Central Pennsylvania and online. He lives in Harrisburg.

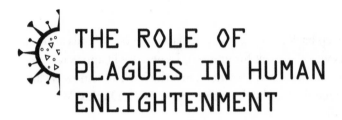

THE ROLE OF PLAGUES IN HUMAN ENLIGHTENMENT

BY MARK CARLSON

WE HAVE ALL heard the phrase, "Avoid it like the plague." It is such a commonplace expression we hardly ever consider its origin. In a way, it may be one of the oldest and most profound idioms in the history of humanity. Yet as with every proverbial dark cloud, there is a silver lining. Sometimes the worst disasters can lead to great good.

Once upon a time, a collection of modern, prosperous nations were interconnected by trade, business, and travel that thrived in a dynamic economy. After several years of good crops and harvests, people were living longer, and the population was rising. Good times appeared to be here to stay.

Then there was a change in the weather. Winters were longer with extreme cold. With years of rainy summers, the crops began to fail. There were food shortages and famine. Business and commerce suffered, further weakening the once-thriving economy. With less food and money, people tightened their belts. In this state, they were utterly vulnerable to attack.

From eastern Asia, an invader brought fear, sickness, and death. The invader was invisible, and no one understood its nature. Within weeks thousands were dying, often within a few days. Every home, every town, and nation were vulnerable to the deadly invader. As the months passed and the death toll rose, soon there were not enough living to bury the dead. They were buried in mass graves or burned in huge pyres.

While this may sound chillingly familiar to our generation, we do not have any direct memory of it. It happened nearly seven hundred years ago in 1347 in Medieval Europe. The invader was a bacillus called bubonic plague. The first recorded outbreak struck the Eastern Roman Byzantine Empire in the sixth century, resulting in over twenty million deaths. Eight centuries later, the bubonic plague struck again, bringing even more devastation. Its origin was Mongolia, arriving in the Mediterranean via the Black Sea on ships carrying spices, silk, wool, and other goods from Asia to Europe.

From trading ports in Greece, Italy, and southern France, the plague swept like wildfire from shops to homes, from villages to towns, in every nation from Italy to Sweden. At least forty million people, a third of the population, died. In terms of percentages, it was the most devastating pandemic in human history. It was known until the mid-nineteenth century as "The Pestilence," then the "Black Death."

The Medieval era was a time when physicians could do little more than treat broken limbs or stomach ailments. Bloodletting, leeches, and herbs were the norm for the so-called healers of the Middle Ages. No one understood or could even comprehend an invisible bacterium that could kill strong and healthy men and women in mere days. Even worse, no one understood the method of transmission of infection. This was a time when most houses had open cesspools, and piles of animal dung littered the streets. Dogs, cats, rats, and pigs freely roamed the towns of central Europe. Personal and public hygiene was virtually nonexistent, and the average human lifespan was rarely beyond the age of fifty. People died from tooth decay and simple infections from cuts and abrasions. A flea bite was so typical as to be unnoticed. But fleas were the vector that spread the bubonic plague to tens of millions of people across the Middle East and Europe. A bite from an infected flea manifested itself with flu-like symptoms in days, followed by painful, ugly inflamed black rings and boils in the crotch and armpits. From that point on, death from respiratory failure was virtually inevitable. Entire families and communities were decimated. No one was safe. It killed the rich and poor, learned and illiterate, merchant and tradesman, aged and young, pious and secular, noble and peasant. But by 1351, the worst was over, and the horror of the Pestilence passed into the memory of the survivors.

According to historian and author James Burke, the 1347 to 1351 bubonic plague pandemic had an extraordinary and unexpected effect on the course of history. Having lived through a biological disaster, Europeans became the pioneers of a new age. The dead had left their property and land to their descendants, and the survivors made use of their sudden prosperity. Still blissfully ignorant of the causes of the plague, those who had lived went on what could only be called a "spending spree." While it might seem immature from the perspective of history, the wild abandon of buying was a celebration of life. Luxury goods like new clothes and fine upholstery appeared all over Europe in the decades after the plague. The wealthy indulged in silks embroidered with silver and gold thread, while the middle-class bought wool and velvet. Even more popular, thanks to cheap flax, linen was soon under every girl's skirt, under every coat, and on every bed. Then as now, when the linen showed signs of wear, it was discarded. That was where one of the long-vanished icons of the Medieval period entered the picture. The man who had gone from home to home to collect bones for fertilizer, the so-called bone man, began collecting old linen and became the rag and bone man.

Once the discarded fabric had been shredded with a knife, it was soaked for forty-eight hours in water and pounded with triphammers powered by the most important prime mover of the Middle Ages, the water wheel. Emerging as a thick pasty white sludge, it was collected on a fine wire mesh. Then along with scores of similar layers between sheets of felt, the pulp was squeezed under a large press to remove the water and dried.

The result was, as we still call it today, rag paper. Superior to wood pulp paper, rag paper was far cheaper than vellum or parchment, both of which came from animal intestines. For centuries scribes and recorders often had to recycle their sheets to minimize costs. Now rag paper was cheap and abundant. But the Black Death had killed off many of the bookkeepers and clerks who had kept records of births, death, property, taxes, court decisions, contracts, and bank accounts. The survivors were overworked and expensive to hire.

The last link in the chain was the 1452 invention of movable type by Johann Gutenberg in Mainz, Germany. Gutenberg changed the world by reducing the time and cost of printing by four hundred times. Within twenty years of 1452, there were hundreds of traveling printers and print shops all over Europe. The same land devastated by the bubonic plague experienced prosperity and an upsurge in literacy, knowledge, and science. The proliferation of printed books opened the way to the most dynamic periods in human understanding, the Renaissance, Reformation, and Enlightenment. From there, the modern world emerged. Although over a century had passed from the end of the Black Death and the advent of mass printing, there is a direct lineage between the two events. Two more epidemics struck Europe in 1665 and 1720, again resulting in vast numbers of dead. An upsurge in the population and renewed prosperity followed each one.

But the bubonic plague was not the only disease that had a profoundly positive effect on history. Even as late as the nineteenth century, medical science was still woefully ignorant of the causes of bacterial spread. In the case of cholera, which causes death through massive diarrhea and dehydration, almost fifteen thousand people died in London in 1832 and 1847. No one understood that raw human waste carrying the cholera bacteria was leaking from sewers and seeping into the soil and contaminating the outmoded water system. Yet as in the Middle Ages, the Victorian Age medical community refused to consider that invisible microbes could cause the epidemic, instead insisting that it came from the stink from the polluted Thames. The fact that the highest number of deaths were in London's most impoverished neighborhoods was another reason to support the "miasma theory."

It was not until the Broad Street epidemic of 1854 that a physician named John Snow, working with a local clergyman named Henry Whitehead, began studying how the London water and sewer systems were the root cause of the epidemic. Victorian England was the first to use statistics and demographics to understand and track how the disease progressed. Snow's work proved that London's woefully primitive wooden and brick sewers were leaking and contaminating the public pumps used by London's poor neighborhoods.

Snow's theory was borne out when the Broad Street pump was shut down, and cholera deaths dropped almost to zero. Parliament finally passed massive legislation to eliminate the source of the epidemics. London's most respected civil engineer, Joseph Bazalget, oversaw the construction of efficient sewers and water treatment plants. Paris and other major cities that had experienced cholera epidemics followed suit. These changes coincided with Louis Pasteur's work in microbiology and Joseph Lister's efforts in sterile surgery, further reducing the death toll from infections and childbirth. The work of Florence Nightingale during the Crimean War also forced the ultra-conservative medical community to change the procedures of caring for soldiers wounded in battle.

In his landmark book *The Ghost Map*, Steven Johnson cited Snow's work as the turning point in the study of epidemiology. Although another half-century would pass before science was able to determine how bacterial infections spread, it was in the nineteenth century that the first real strides in public health and sanitation were made. Again, this serves to illustrate how humanity has prospered and grown despite terrible and shattering biological crises.

Today we are still learning, but the human need to know and understand catastrophe has always been one of the most significant catalysts of social change and improvement.

⟦ SOURCES ⟧

Burke, J. (1978) *Connections, An Alternative View of Change.* Chapter 7, Faith in Numbers. Little, Brown & Co, New York.

Gies, F. (1994) *Cathedral, Forge and Waterwheel - Technology and Invention in the Middle Ages.* Chapter 6, The High Middle Ages, 1200 to 1500, Cloth, Paper and Banking. Harper Collins, New York, New York.

Johnson, S. (2016) *The Ghost Map: The Story of London's Most Terrifying Epidemic.* Penguin Group, New York, New York.

Kantor, N. (2001) *The Wake of the Plague – The Black Death and the World it Made.* New York Free Pres, New York, New York.

Kelly, J. (2005) *The Great Mortality: An Intimate History of the Black Death, 1st Edition.* Harper Collins, New York, New York.

⟦ ABOUT THE AUTHOR ⟧ --

MARK CARLSON is a military historian and contributor to more than twenty national magazines. Legally blind, he works with the aid of talking software. He is the author of three books, the latests of which is *The Marines' Lost Squadron - The Odyssey of VMF-422*, published by Sunbury Press. Carlson is a past president of Toastmasters and a popular public speaker. He lives in San Diego with his wife Jane.

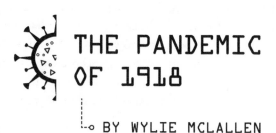

THE PANDEMIC OF 1918

⌐o BY WYLIE MCLALLEN

AS THE GREAT War in Europe came to an end in the fall of 1918, the Americans who had fought in the trenches with the Allies against Germany had lived through brutal conditions that could not have seemed worse. But earlier in the year, a virus began spreading that very briefly at first appeared no more dangerous than a common cold. The influenza of that season, however, was far more dangerous than a cold. A viral disease caused by a deadly strain of avian influenza, the 1918 Spanish Flu remains the most severe pandemic in modern history. In the two years that this scourge ravaged the earth, at least a fifth of the world's population was infected, almost half a billion people, with the death toll estimated as high as fifty million. It was first thought to be caused by bacteria, and the vaccines scientists tried to develop based upon this thinking were, of course, ineffectual. Scientists knew about viruses, but without powerful modern microscopes, a virus had not yet been seen, and with little known about the spread through droplets in one's breath, the Spanish Flu quickly circled the globe.

It spread in waves following the paths of its human carriers along trade routes and shipping lanes. Outbreaks swept through North America, Europe, Asia, Africa, Brazil, and the South Pacific; most of humanity felt the deadly effects of this respiratory virus. Although there is no universal consensus regarding the virus's origin, there is some thought that it originated in China in a rare genetic shift of the influenza virus. The recombination of its surface proteins created a virus novel to almost everyone and a loss of herd immunity. India had an exceptionally high mortality rate, with about five deaths per one-hundred people. The Great War, with its mass movements of young men in armies and aboard ships, aided the rapid diffusion and attack, creating an unusually high mortality rate among healthy young adults, a unique feature of the pandemic. As the colossal war raged with millions of young men packed together on ships and in trenches and on the fields, the spread of influenza on both sides caused more death than their weapons. The disease became known as the "Spanish Flu" because Spain, as a neutral country, did not impose wartime censorship, unlike the Allies and Central Powers, and so its newspapers reported in detail the grave effects of the epidemic and these widespread stories created a false impression that Spain was the epicenter.

The first wave of influenza in the United States appeared in military posts in the early spring of 1918. Though a sign of what was to come, amid a war, few paid any attention to these early outbreaks in the training camps. By the fall, when the death rate could no longer be ignored, this lack of initial action was criticized. Of the U.S. soldiers who died in Europe, half of them fell to the flu virus rather than the enemy. Returning soldiers coming together brought the virus with them and to those they contacted, creating a second wave of the epidemic, this time infecting civilians, killing almost 200,000 Americans in October of 1918 alone. At the end of the war, November 11, 1918, as people celebrated Armistice Day with parades and large parties, an even greater rebirth of the epidemic occurred in some cities, infecting millions of people that winter with the flu. An estimated 675,000 Americans died of influenza during the pandemic, ten times as many as in the world war.

Hospital facilities and staff were stretched to the limit. There was a shortage of physicians, many lost in military service, and many lost to the epidemic, leaving mostly medical students to care for the sick. The Red Cross created a National Committee on Influenza to mobilize all forces to fight the Spanish Flu. Emergency hospitals were created. In some areas of the country, the nursing shortage was so acute that local businesses were asked to allow workers a day off if they volunteered in the hospitals at night. A nurse serving at the Naval Hospital in Great Lakes, Illinois, described what happened there and in many hospitals around the country: "The morgues were packed almost to the ceiling with bodies stacked one on top of another. The morticians worked day and night. You could never turn around without seeing a big red truck loaded with caskets for the train station so bodies could be sent home. We didn't have time to treat them. We didn't take temperatures; we didn't even have time to take blood pressure. We would give them a little hot whiskey toddy; that's about all we had time to do. They would have terrific nosebleeds with it. Sometimes the blood would just shoot across the room. You had to get out of the way, or someone's nose would bleed all over you." The "new sciences" of infectious agents and immunology raced to come up with a vaccine or therapy to stop the rapid, deadly spread.

The first symptoms would come on suddenly, sharp debilitating pain in the back or joints followed by dizziness and fever and chills, then the onset of pneumonia, and with no antibiotics yet to ward it off, the skin would likely turn blue as it went cyanotic. Finally, when the lungs filled with enough fluid, a patient would drown in their bed. There are stories of people on their way to work suddenly becoming sick and dying within hours. One physician wrote that patients would rapidly "develop the most vicious type of pneumonia that has ever been seen," and later, "it is simply a struggle for air until they suffocate." Physicians were helpless. Bodies piled up as the massive deaths ensued. Besides the lack of healthcare workers and medical supplies, there was a shortage of coffins, morticians, and gravediggers. With no vaccine to protect against influenza infection and no antibiotics to treat secondary bacterial infections that can be associated with influenza infections, control efforts worldwide were limited to non-pharmaceutical interventions such as isolation, quarantine, good personal hygiene, use of disinfectants, and limitations of public gatherings, which were applied unevenly.

Those lucky enough to avoid infection had to deal with public ordinances to restrain the spread of the disease. As people had submitted to the strict measures and loss of freedom during the war, they accepted the new theories the medical and scientific communities applied to the prevention, diagnostics, and treatment of influenza. In the absence of a vaccine, public health interventions were the first line of defense. These measures included closing schools, shops, and restaurants, restrictions on transportation, mandating physical distancing, and banning public gatherings. Getting citizens to comply with these orders was difficult; a health officer in San Francisco shot three people when one refused to wear a mandatory face mask, in Arizona, police handed out $10 fines to those caught without protective gear; but eventually, these measures paid off. Implementing strict closures and controls on public gatherings in major cities cut transmission rates by 30 to 50 percent. New York City, which reacted earliest to the crisis with mandatory quarantines and staggered business hours, experienced the lowest death rate on the Eastern Seaboard. This allowed time for vaccine development and lessened the strain on health care systems. But relaxing intervention measures too early could cause an otherwise stabilized city to relapse. St. Louis was so emboldened by its low death rate that restrictions were lifted on public gathering, and a rash of new cases soon followed. Cities that kept restrictions in place did not experience high death rates in a second wave of the epidemic. Studies then found that the key to flattening the curve was physical distancing, which likely remains true a century later in the current battle against coronavirus.

A third less-lethal wave followed in January 1919, ending in the spring. One particular case would have an extraordinary impact on history. On April 3, 1919, during the Versailles Peace Conference, Woodrow Wilson collapsed. His sudden weakness and severe confusion halfway through that conference— widely commented upon—very possibly contributed to his abandoning the peacetime principles of his Fourteen Point address. The result was the disastrous peace treaty, which, within a generation, would contribute to the start of World War II. Some historians have attributed Wilson's confusion to a minor stroke. In fact, he had a 103-degree temperature, intense coughing fits, diarrhea, and other severe symptoms. A stroke explains none of the symptoms. Influenza, which was then widespread in Paris and killed a young aide to Wilson, explains all of them—including his confusion. Experts would later agree that many patients afflicted by the pandemic influenza had cognitive or psychological symptoms. As an authoritative 1927 medical review concluded, "There is no doubt that the neuropsychiatric effects of influenza are profound . . . hardly second to its effect on the respiratory system."

Scientists and other experts are still asking questions about the virus and the devastation it caused, including why the second wave was so much more lethal than the first. Some argue that the first wave was caused by an ordinary seasonal influenza virus that was different from the pandemic virus; but the evidence seems overwhelming that the pandemic virus had both a mild and virulent form, caus- ing mild as well as severe outbreaks, and then, for reasons that remain unclear, the virulent form of the virus became more common. After that third wave, the 1918 virus did not go away, but it did lose its extraordinary lethality, partly because many human immune systems now recognized it and partly because it lost the ability to easily invade the lungs. No longer a bloodthirsty murderer, it evolved into seasonal influenza.

Since 1918, there have been several other influenza pandemics, although none as deadly. A flu pandemic from 1957 to 1958 killed around 2 million people worldwide, including some 70,000 people in the United States, and a pandemic from 1968 to 1969 killed approximately 1 million people, including some 34,000

Americans. The current COVID-19 pandemic is a deadly and frightening scourge, but this time we know a lot more about viruses and how to curb their spread.

⟦ SOURCES ⟧

Editors, www.cdc.gov/flu/pandemic-resources/1918-pandemic.

Editors, Spanish Flu, History.com.

Editors, Spanish Flu: the deadliest pandemic in history, www.livescience.com.

John M. Barry, *The New York Times*, March 17, 2020, The single most important lesson from the 1918 Influenza.

Molly Billings, *The Influenza Pandemic of 1918*, Stanford University.

Nina Strochlic and Riley D. Campine, *National Geographic*, How some cities 'flattened the curve' during the 1918 flu pandemic.

⟦ ABOUT THE AUTHOR ⟧

WYLIE MCLALLEN grew up in Memphis, Tennessee. He studied fiction and composition at the University of Tennessee under Robert Drake, who was a close friend of author Flannery O'Conner. He is the author of *Tigers by the River*, a history of early pro football published by The Sunbury Press.

HOW ARE FUTURE PANDEMICS LIKELY TO BE DIFFERENT?

BY THOMAS M. MALAFARINA

WORLD WAR III has begun. But for the first time, mankind is not at war with his fellow man. Countries are too busy battling an unseen enemy, a bug, a germ a virus known as COVID-19. How this war will end remains to be seen. How many lives will be lost, and when those who survive do so, how will the world prepare for the next pandemic? And rest assured, there will, beyond any doubt, be a next pandemic.

Pandora's box had been open, and the world has been forced to make one of those monumental paradigm shifts, one which can never be undone. At the time of this writing, the COVID-19 virus is in full pandemic swing, killing thousands of people worldwide, with no cure, no vaccine, and no end in sight.

The governments of the world have forced their populations into complete mandatory lockdown for the first time in modern history, in an attempt to prevent the death toll from reaching into the millions. At the risk of sounding overly pessimistic, it's quite possible that by the time this work is published, I or several of the other authors in the collection might have already caught the virus, and a few may have succumbed to the dreaded disease. At present, I am healthy and well. But things change daily if not hourly in this particular war. So, for the record, if I happen to fall among the victims, feel free to publish this posthumously. Sound a bit melodramatic? Two months ago I would have agreed, but after all I've seen in the past several weeks, not so much.

The powers that be have come up with the term "shelter in place" to try to make staying quarantined in your home for weeks on end more palatable, but the word that has become more prevalent to describe the situation is "lockdown." At first, we were told the lockdown would be for two weeks, then four. As of the end of March, it was determined that the lockdown will continue until the end of April at the earliest. And the bodies keep piling up.

Most of the country's businesses, which have been deemed "non-life sustaining," have been forced to close their doors, putting unprecedented millions out of work. The stock market has taken a nosedive, which cost investors trillions of dollars. The long-term effect on the economy remains to be seen, even with proposed government stimulus checks forthcoming. Schools, churches, restaurants, bars, anywhere people gather have been closed. Airplanes have been grounded, not by government mandate but by consumer fears. Highways are as empty as the shelves of grocery stores were during the height of the initial panic buying.

We have instituted something called "social distancing," which means you stay a minimum of six feet from anyone. We no longer shake hands, hug, or come into any physical contact on those rare occasions when we see people we know. Many of us have not seen or hugged our children or grandchildren since this all began. We can leave our homes to buy what groceries and supplies remain, or to walk our dogs. But then we must return to our homes and shelter in place like frightened rabbits.

Some people whose employers are permitted to stay open can work from home if possible. Others, such as myself, (I am in the military defense manufacturing industry) must travel to our jobs, doing our best to avoid others. To quote the title of the 1980s band REM's song, "It's The End Of The World As We Know It."

On the optimistic side, however, and although it might not sound so—I am a hopeless optimist—when, not if we survive this pandemic, how will we handle future outbreaks? New precedents have been set and continue to be set daily. We are fighting in an uncharted wilderness, and many of the things we thought of as stable aspects of life no longer exist. The rulebook has gone up in flames. Humanity was caught off guard and sucker-punched. Fool me once, shame on you; fool me twice, shame on me. We won't let it happen again.

Whenever the germ-infested dust settles, those of us remaining will be putting stopgap measures into place to be ready for the next pandemic. On the individual level, I suspect people will begin buying in bulk like never before. Basements will be lined with shelves full of non-perishable goods in preparation for the next lockdown. Those people who formerly scoffed at warehouse shopping club members, who on a regular basis filled their carts with jumbo bundles of paper towels, tissues, and toilet paper, will be rushing to buy club memberships. Homes will all have designated areas for such items.

Stores on the other hand, will likely be mandated by law to instantly put restrictions on how many of a certain item can be purchased during a time of crises, preventing such ridiculous catastrophes like the great toilet paper rush of 2020. If I live through this and live on to a ripe old age, I'll never figure that one out. Toilet paper? Honestly?

But what else? Suppose a new superbug hits, and we are fortunate enough to have a vaccine for it. What about the "anti-vaccine" crowd? If they get sick, will they be refused treatment? Will they be allowed to be the reason the virus spreads, or will they be forced to take the vaccine? If they are forced to vaccinate and can prove an adverse or allergic reaction to the vaccine will they have legal recourse? If they refuse to vaccinate, will they be put into detainment facilities? This may sound unimaginable or something from a science fiction story, but these are all possibilities that could actually take place—perhaps even before this book is published. Things are changing that quickly.

And what about businesses? How will they change to adapt to this brave new world? More people will be telecommuting for sure, but the Internet will most definitely have to be beefed up to handle the new traffic. We are currently experiencing major bandwidth problems during this crisis because of the additional internet activity.

Will "non-life sustaining" businesses be mandated to put together catastrophic savings accounts as part of an employee's benefit to cover their salaries and medical needs if they are forced to shelter at home for the next pandemic? Or might this take the form of a new type of catastrophic insurance policy, which employers will be required to purchase? Mark my words, once we've survived this and "shelter in place" has been proven to be successful, there will be future lockdowns.

During this current crisis, I've seen home centers, grocery, and convenience stores, as well as medical facilities, turned into something out of a bad 1960s sci-fi movie. I never thought in my lifetime that I would be standing in line (the mandatory 6 feet "social distancing" space from anyone else), and I would hear a disembodied emotionless robotic prerecorded voice come over the intercom saying, "Welcome to our store. Your health and safety are our priority. Please maintain social distancing at all times, remember to wash your hands—and have a pleasant shopping experience."

Another store required me to approach a folding table where I was made to apply hand sanitizer before entering the main part of the store. Then I was required to be escorted around the store by one of the staff. If more than six people showed up, they had to wait in line for the next available employees. (maintaining social distancing of course). At the checkout counter, I was required to place my items on the counter then immediately step behind a plexiglass partition so as not to potentially infect the counter clerk. I understand and realize such precautions are necessary, but it's all so surrealistic for me, and I write horror fiction, so that speaks volumes. Remember, this is not science fiction; this is reality today. I can only imagine what the future will hold.

Perhaps our governments will next demand that citizens receive read/write data chip implants, containing history of past and recent vaccinations. This chip could be scanned as the person entered a facility, and if the person was deemed to be not within government mandated standards for immunity, they could be refused entry. This might be utilized at non-life sustaining stores' offices and other such places of employment as well, to allow them to stay open during times of pandemic while protecting employees as well as the general public.

Such a chip could feed back information such as temperature, heart rate, and blood pressure so it could be analyzed for the employee's overall health and condition before permitting admittance. It might be capable of checking for indicators of potential drug or alcohol abuse as well.

Although I am not advocating the use of such a device, I can honestly say I could see it happening someday. People are more than willing to give up their rights and freedoms for a sense of safety and well-being, whether real or imagined. A month ago, I would have said it was impossible. Then again, many of the things I've seen during this pandemic I never would have believed I'd see in my lifetime.

There are so many other areas which will see significant change, including education, health, recreation, entertainment, transportation, and gatherings of any kind involving groups of people. As this war drags on, the world beyond 2020 will no longer resemble the world of just three months ago. It already does not, and this is just the beginning. There are many more significant changes, which will imminently be coming for the world to be ready for the next pandemic.

C ABOUT THE AUTHOR]

THOMAS M. MALAFARINA (www.ThomasMMalafarina.com) has published seven horror novels, as well as six collections of horror short stories. He has also published a book of often strange single panel cartoons. All of his books have been published through Hellbender Books an imprint of Sunbury Press. (www.Sunburypress.com).

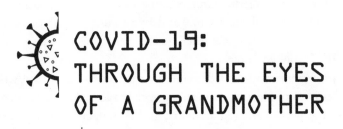

COVID-19: THROUGH THE EYES OF A GRANDMOTHER

BY BARBARA MATTHEWS

COVID-19 IS BUT one more point on the timeline of my life. One more "unprecedented" point, that is. God—how I have come to despise that word!

Understanding how I feel is complicated. I suspect it is for all of you. Perceptions and opinions are generally based on past histories and how we use them to plan. That seems to be damned near impossible with coronavirus—so I take it one day at a time.

In trying to comprehend the incomprehensible, I have had to look back over the past seventy years. How did history get us here? What did we learn? Can we use past experiences to formulate strategies today? What do we value? How do we prioritize which factors are most important? What will be relevant to younger generations?

HISTORICAL INFLUENCES

Every generation has characteristics developed in response to what is going on in their world. The Depression and World Wars were major formative factors for the "Greatest Generation," so named for their remarkable determination and perseverance. My generation, the Baby Boomers, were born during a time of relative peace and prosperity. I think it is safe to say that life in the 1950s was a simpler time than it had been for our parents and grandparents. Our folks wanted to provide us with more opportunities and a better life. They raised us following the guidelines of Dr. Benjamin Spock, an American pediatrician who wrote *Baby and Child Care*, considered to be the bible of child-rearing.

It is conjectured that Spock's philosophy spawned the cultural transformation or "counterculture" of the 1960s. He was later criticized for allegedly propagating permissiveness and an expectation of instant gratification that led disaffected young people to adopt alternative "hippie" lifestyles. These behaviors, which were in sharp contrast to our parent's near-absolute standards of right and wrong, were the foundation for the "generation gap" and led to the Baby Boomer generation being defined by "sex, drugs, and rock n' roll."

The counterculture movement began in earnest with the assassination of President Kennedy and gained momentum with both the African American Civil Rights and Women's Rights Movements. It became revolutionary with the expansion of our government's extensive involvement in Vietnam and was exacerbated by the assassinations of Martin Luther King and Bobby Kennedy. For me, the climax of that era occurred on May 4, 1970, with the Kent State shootings. The death and injuries of those students on my college campus became the catalyst for me to change.

Boomers began to marry and have kids. Women were entering the workforce in droves, wanting their lives to be more fulfilling than just being wives and mothers. Divorce increased, resulting in more single-parent households. Gen-X children, who often came home to empty houses, were known as latchkey kids. Over the 70s and 80s, the economy was dogged by high inflation, business slowdowns, rising unemployment, the oil crisis, and declining government revenues. High unemployment, tax cuts, and the trickledown economy resulted in growing national debt.

But in the 90s, the World Wide Web spurred the economy to steady growth, low unemployment, and minimal inflation. However, that wealth also began to concentrate into fewer hands. Other than the Three Mile Island nuclear incident in the Harrisburg area, there did not seem to be as many "Where-were-you-when" events of previous generations.

GEN-X COMES OF AGE

September 11, 2001, is a date I need not explain. Like December 7, 1941, the day has gone down in infamy. I want to address what ensued from that catastrophe, in addition to other tragedies that occurred in the weeks, months, and years to follow. These events shook the foundation upon which my outlook on life is built, as I am sure it did for most other Americans, as well. The sadness of those days was prolonged by other signs of sickness in our society.

On September 18, 2001, an anthrax attack occurred in the United States, which lasted for several weeks as letters containing anthrax spores were mailed to several news media offices and two Democratic U.S. Senators. Five people were killed and seventeen others infected. Later, there was a series of coordinated shootings that took place over three weeks in October of 2002. People were shot while filling up their gas tanks in Maryland, Virginia, and Washington, D.C.

These atrocities were personalized for me by the fact that my oldest daughter was living in Annapolis at that time. Since she married, I had begun looking forward to someday having grandchildren. But daily life in our country felt so unstable and insecure; I began to wonder if my children should even bring off-spring into this world. My thinking was taking on a defeatist, fatalistic bend.

But then, I thought, "Why shouldn't my kids have the same opportunities for fulfillment as I have had?" The answer to that was, of course, they should. As the next dozen years unfolded, they did just that as they brought a new generation of nine little beings into our family and our world.

THE RUMBLINGS

Fifty years ago, my greatest ambition in life was to have a family of my own. I wanted to replicate what I had as a child before my innocence was crushed by the weight of the world that bore down on me as an adolescent and teen. When I married and had children, the conditions were not ideal, and the odds were long, but somehow, I persevered. Forty years later, I had a deep sense of satisfaction that my job was well done. I was proud of the people my children had become—good parents and good providers. For a time, I thought, "These are my favorite years as a parent." I was able to bask in the warm glow of my "success" without having to shoulder the responsibility. The grandchildren were my reward.

But over the past several years, satisfaction is again being supplanted by uneasiness. Life is changing—as it always has, but now, because of technology, it changes so *fast*. I fear that in the event life as we know it takes a dramatic turn, today's younger generations may not have the foundation to rebuild our society. We all know technology is a powerful tool. But technology has also increased our vulnerability. I wonder: "Has modern society been built upon a house of cards?

I think it is a given that grandparents want to feel relevant—that their wisdom and experience will be of benefit to their grandchildren. But honestly? Baby Boomers have never experienced what it is like to be a kid in today's technological world. The playbook has changed.

I certainly want to feel useful and able to make contributions of consequence. But whereas Gen-X has their feet in both worlds, we grandparents do not. Being on the leading edge of the Baby Boomer generation, I am officially a senior citizen. I recently discovered that the meaning of "Baby Boomer" has morphed. To today's tweens and teens, the term—once synonymous with rebellious sex, drugs, and rock n' roll—now means "a technologically challenged old person." While our parents became known as "the greatest generation," mine has been reduced to this! A bitter pill to swallow.

OUT OF NOWHERE: THE COVID-19 CRISIS

Concerns for my grandchildren's futures began to smolder well-before I had even heard of COVID-19. Many factors threaten us, such as global warming, gun violence, social inequality, and insufficient healthcare. Since the 1990s, our government has been increasingly crippled by a "my-way-or-the-highway" approach that has near paralyzed our government's ability to legislate. Even worse, the *people* have become so polarized that at any given time, at least half of the population feels disenfranchised. The country is being torn to shreds. We are vulnerable to foreign enemies. Our democracy is threatened.

Indeed, the entire world is a tinderbox and COVID-19 the flame. It feels apocalyptic. It has become easy to envision a post-apocalyptic America, as described by Cormac McCarthy in *The Road*, without electricity, running water, or even humanity—where people will do anything to survive.

With COVID-19 now upon us, I find that my children, and the children of my peers, are taking over a new role. "Don't you think we need to start practicing social distancing?" my youngest daughter asked. Since seniors are at high risk, she is worried about me getting the virus. I would not want her to feel responsible for my death if I were to succumb. So, now our children are actively assuming the position of "generation in charge."

After my daughter's remark, the first thought that crossed my mind was: "If I get coronavirus and die, I will never be in the same room or be able to hug my children and grandchildren again." Morose, I know, but this is a scenario that is happening every day.

Of all my concerns, one has made it to the top of my list of apprehensions. All I really want is to see my grandchildren (meaning their generation and successive generations) have the opportunity for a good future. Everything else falls in place behind that.

IN QUEST OF OPTIMISM

I am thankful that Gen-X is rising to this occasion and proud to have been a part of raising such a competent, self-trained, and resourceful generation. Baby Boomers have had their share of trepidation over the years for leaving their children unattended as latchkey kids. But it now appears that Gen-X children developed lower expectations of being taken care of, and therefore learned how to fend for themselves. Since the turn of the millennium, Gen-X has lived through tragedies and epidemics—and have developed the ability to handle life's tough moments by using their coping skills and by developing new ones. Like their grandparents, they are resilient and able to persevere—handling the current status quo without complaint. Gen-X is self-sufficient and does not hesitate to take on responsibility. They know how to stay entertained and multi-task to combat boredom and solitude. They are empathetic, provide calm, and follow the rules. Since Gen-X remembers life without technology, they know how to adapt and make accommodations to bear burdens and resist fear.

How my Gen-X kids adapted creatively this week:
▶ Arranged a family get-together on Zoom
▶ Played Scattegories on FaceTime
▶ Used FaceTime for Grandma to tutor

For many Americans, the scale of the coronavirus catastrophe calls to mind the crises of the past—those events that reshaped society in lasting ways. We are, after all, Americans with "can do" attitudes:
▶ We will get through this
▶ This too shall pass
▶ We will find our way

I have always found it preferable to know what I am dealing with without withering from hard, cold reality. But that approach does not preclude recognizing and acknowledging the positives. Here are some that I have observed occurring daily:
1. Connecting with family
   ➤ Moratorium on youth team sports; more unstructured family-time
   ➤ Visiting long-distance via FaceTime
   ➤ Walking, biking and playing together

2. Connecting with neighbors
   - Outdoor-at-a-distance chats
   - Altruism—more caring about our fellow man
3. Less procrastination
   - Cleaning and decluttering
   - Confronting tasks; preparing for contingencies
4. Developing efficiencies, shopping online
5. Seeking and sharing in-home entertainment ideas

But this is just a start. Preserving the American standard and moving ahead requires 1) examining, reconsidering, and confronting our obstacles; 2) addressing them as a united front while recognizing our core American values, and 3) establishing common goals to rediscover the better version of ourselves.

COVID-19: A CATALYST FOR CHANGE?

It is a sure thing. The pandemic will cause immense pain and suffering. Therefore, we can no longer accept the status quo, which brought us to a virtual standstill and ripe for COVID-19 to plunder. Understand that society as we know it will change one way or another. Recognize that crisis moments are motivators for change, and that inflexibility will keep us on the path to tragedy. Different people have different priorities. I have been thinking about these:

We live in a global society. As people who share this planet Earth, we cannot live in isolation or care only about ourselves. Multilateral diplomacy, including cooperation with allies and adversaries alike, is imperative when dealing with global problems such as climate change and viral pandemics. The shock of COVID-19 is increasing momentum for change and improving the climate for constructive dialogue. Ethical and effective leaders understand that public trust is crucial to governing and that gaining trust is dependent on telling the truth.

Overcome the polarization that exists within our country. The government today is no longer about "We the People" as a *whole*. The time is right for Americans to look past their differences and to fight the common enemy so that we can find our way back to this core principle.

We were founded on democracy; it is what makes us special, but we are dangerously close to losing its inherent freedoms. Shame on those who demonstrate the willingness to forfeit our democratic principals to achieve their narrow-minded and selfish goals. These behaviors are making this crisis more dangerous than it needs to be.

Voter suppression is a problem in our country that could potentially disappear as a result of the coronavirus. As election officials adopt new ways to allow for safer voting during a pandemic, they will also be creating more options to facilitate voting permanently. Higher voter turnout results in fewer disenfranchised citizens; it has the potential to transform partisan competition in America.

Social policies are gaining priority as an outgrowth of COVID-19 strategies. With increasing awareness of the disproportionate impact on minority communities, public health and education services are in greater demand. Stop worshiping money and giving it the power to influence every decision to be made for the good of the people. Being the richest does not mean being the best. Coronavirus is an equalizer. It may enable us to relearn how to enjoy the simplicities of life and remind us that material things are not what makes us genuinely happy.

Expertise matters. As a result of the coronavirus, Americans will once again tune into our core values; respect our scientific, security, and government professionals; and realize that our institutions have been established to support the functions of our democracy and to deal with a crisis.

Use technology to our advantage, not to our detriment. Online communication may be a boon to connecting with family and friends, but it can also minimize meaningful communication and create dangerous connections. The use of technology facilitates our ability to educate our children and allows employees to work from home during the coronavirus. These changes may lessen the resistance to innovative change in our long-established systems. The flexibility these technologies provides will go a long way in dealing with educational costs, family care, and commuting.

IMAGINE ...

Generations are about cultural change. Baby Boomers influenced the world with their youthful idealism and their questioning of established authority systems. As they transitioned to the greater responsibilities of adulthood, they became strongly career- and achievement-oriented. How this led our country to the point of paralysis, I am unclear. I am clear that we created a mess for our children to clean up, and that the time is ripe for the next generation to assume the yoke of authority.

It is an enigma what role Millennials and Gen-Z will play. There is much conjecture about the characteristics of these up-and-coming generations, but I do not think we know enough yet to envision their potential. Millennials and Gen-Z make up nearly half of the U.S. population, which will enhance their political influence if they mobilize. These generations have delayed the "adult" behaviors like sex, smoking, drinking, and driving—mostly beneficial. They grew up in the digital age—Gen-Z exclusively—which makes them well-equipped to navigate technology. Young people exhibit less focus and shorter attention spans, making them susceptible to information overload. However, they also have better-developed aptitudes to multi-task. Millennials and Gen-Z are obsessed with information since it is so readily available. They have more education and job equality. They are also compulsive about sharing feelings and experiences via social media, spending more "virtual" time with people, and learning about people all over the world. Therefore, they are more accepting of equality and diversity.

The problems created by the virus did not flourish in isolation—they took root in fertile soil prepared beforehand. If we are to survive the pandemic and come out better on the other side, we must recognize the opportunity it presents for us to right the wrongs that have developed due to partisan politics, social injustice, and greed.

Since this will not happen overnight, I keep telling my teenaged grandchildren that they need to prepare themselves to take over and right the wrongs of my generation. In the meantime, the Baby Boomers and Gen-Xers will need to look at those characteristics we see as flaws and consider the genuine possibility that these unique traits may be the younger generation's unrecognized strengths. Millennials and Gen-Zs are open-minded and possess the ability to be self-aware while still recognizing the value of diversity. These perspectives on the world are needed to move forward. Youthful potential is not to be taken for granted, for they are, indeed, the future.

[ABOUT THE AUTHOR] --

BARBARA MATTHEWS's career encompassed the fields of adult education and social work. It was both her experience as a Care Manager for the Dauphin County Area Agency on Aging and as a full-time caregiver for her mother-in-law that motivated her to write: *What to Do about Mama? Expectations and Realities of Caregiving.*

Barb has since written her memoirs and a family cookbook, both of which are at least a loose outgrowth of her caregiving experience. She is grateful to have been a part of this COVID-19 project. It has been a means to process a perplexing world.

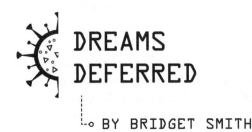

DREAMS DEFERRED

BY BRIDGET SMITH

AS A FAMILY of six, we've seen our share of trying times. Like most, financial difficulties and the stress of a chaotic lifestyle are at the top of the list. And like most parents, we've spent countless hours carting our kids to practices, baseball games, gymnastics meets, and cheer competitions; late-night drives filled with bathroom stops and fast food, sleeping children in the third row of our SUV, and over time, teenagers fighting over control of the music, years spent watching our kids grow up through a rearview mirror. And no matter the toll on our bank accounts and our sanity, we wouldn't trade it for the world. All we wanted was to see our kids achieve their dreams—playing college baseball, becoming a college cheerleader, and graduating from dental school.

Never in a million years could I have guessed what lay ahead. Never would I have believed that these years spent pursuing dreams would come to such a screeching halt. And not from the likeliest of culprits—like being cut from the ball team or missing the mark at cheer tryouts—but from an invisible virus.

For families like us, focused on high school graduations and college applications, so far removed from anything resembling a pandemic, the Coronavirus hit us like a brick to the head. Most of us downplayed the initial panic—at least that was the consensus in my family. This would certainly pass. It was just inconceivable to think that *everything* would cease. But cease it did—and with a vengeance.

They say timing is everything, and for many families in a similar situation, this statement could not have been more real. My oldest daughter—a third-year dental student at the University of Mississippi—was finally spending most of her class time in a clinic. My youngest son, a community college relief pitcher, was just three days shy of the first conference game of the season. And my youngest, a high school senior, was getting ready for spring break and the last Ole Miss cheer clinic before tryouts. Every compass pointed in the right direction; the stars seemed magically aligned. But, alas, "the best-laid plans oft go astray."

The gravity of the situation finally hit home with a frantic phone call from my son.

"Baseball is canceled. Like the whole season," he relayed. "We're all going home."

"No," I said in my most sympathetic, mom's voice. "I think maybe everyone's just being cautious. You'll be back on the field in a few weeks. Just let this pass."

But, of course, things only got worse. By the time that first weekend passed, every school sport had ceased to be. Even MLB cut short spring training and delayed the start of their season. And to top it off, thousands of high school senior and community college baseball players were poised to play those first conference games, show off, and catch the eye of some Division 1 college scouts. For many, this was their last shot. Once we got word that schools would switch to distance learning for the remainder of the semester, we knew it was over—at least for now. The pre-season play would be the last baseball for a while.

And if grieving over baseball wasn't enough, let's not forget my high school senior. When school closures were first announced, the reaction from my daughter and every other high school senior in the country was the same: Spring break was still on! It was like hitting the lottery! But as that first week unfolded, proms were canceled, senior parties were postponed, and finally, graduations were tabled as school systems struggled to revamp the remainder of the school year. For the Class of 2020, the class that was born in the tense months after 9/11, there would be no celebrations, no photo ops, no caps and gowns.

To say these seniors are special is an understatement. Having brought my daughter into that post-9/11 world was trying enough, but to think that she and her classmates across the country will enter the next phase of their lives in yet another time of uncertainty is simply inconceivable. Having life as they knew it ripped out from under them in a matter of days, replaced by social isolation and COVID data, is all too much, even for these tech-savvy fanatics who already spend the majority of their days on social media. Choosing to socialize via Snapchat and Instagram is one thing—having no option is quite another.

But as scary and confusing as these quarantined days may be, my daughter seems hopeful that her future college days will be just as exciting as those of her brothers and sister. We can only pray this will be so. We can only pray that through it all, these young people learn how precious life is and gain a new perspective on the importance of personal freedom. Much like those months after 9/11, we as Americans are facing a new challenge: to adapt to the changing world we live in, and quickly. So too is the Class of 2020, and just as they have prevailed thus far, they will rise to meet that challenge.

Amid trying times, there often lies a great gift. For every college student who packed up early, forced to move back home before that last formal or the start of a baseball season, for every high school student whose senior year was canceled, and for every professional student caught in the uncertainty of an incomplete year, there was an unexpected blessing waiting at home—a time for families like ours to be together again, to enjoy days of eating and laughing, lying on the couch binge-watching Netflix, a time to reacquaint ourselves with the ones we love. During this crisis, children have learned compassion, families have grown stronger, and communities have come together like never before. Social distancing may be the buzz word of the day, and we may be separated from friends and extended family, but in homes across America, the bonds formed during this time have been a blessing.

And so in the next few weeks, my oldest daughter will officially begin her 4th, and final, year of dental school, albeit through distance-learning; my youngest son will complete his sophomore year of college and will move on to the next level of baseball, and my high school senior will receive her diploma in the mail. Although these milestones will be reached without the typical celebration, they will be reached regardless of the circumstances. And maybe *that* is what they will gain out of this crisis—that sense of hope that comes with overcoming obstacles, and a keener sense of the power of the human spirit. To recognize our human limitations—but *never* give up. Maybe *that* is what American families should take from this situation. Blessings really do come in the strangest of forms.

[ABOUT THE AUTHOR] --

BRIDGET SMITH, M.ED. in English, is the author of historical fiction novel *Where Elephants Fought*. She was born in Columbia, Tennessee, and now resides in a quaint Mississippi town with her husband and four children. Bridget has taught English for over twenty years.

COVID-19:
THE GREAT EQUALIZER

⌐o BY IRIS DORBIAN

IT WAS THE dawn of the pandemic, and everyone was under quarantine. But that did not stop a certain aging 1980s pop music icon from waxing philosophical about the democratizing effect of an unprecedented public health crisis while lounging decadently like a modern Marie Antoinette in her sudsy, rose petal-spattered bathtub. "That's the thing about COVID-19," mused Madonna in a video posted to both her Instagram and Twitter accounts, "it doesn't care about how rich you are, how famous you are, how funny you are, how smart you are, where you live, how old you are, what amazing stories you can tell. It's the great equalizer and what's terrible about it is what's great about it."

The irony here, if you can forget the ridiculously over-the-top setting, replete with ominous piano accompaniment or that the Material Girl seemed to be either inebriated or high—she is right. Like any disease, be it a contagion or not, COVID-19 does not discriminate: It will attack anyone, regardless of fame, fortune, or influence. It does not care. In the eyes of the coronavirus, there is no class system, no hierarchy of power or privilege. All are equally susceptible and vulnerable. Your wallet cannot immunize or save you. COVID-19 is the Bolshevik of pandemics.

In a strangely perverse way—and Madonna alluded to this in her bathtub ramblings—there was something weirdly comforting knowing we were all in this together. COVID-19 united us in this crucible of fear and manic preparedness. Every day, every minute, we were fed this daily mantra of coronavirus prevention, courtesy of the Centers for Disease Control and Prevention: Wash your hands frequently, maintain social distance, don't touch your face, stay home, etc.[1] Seeing late-night TV hosts like Stephen Colbert continue production from home while interviewing quarantined celebrity guests via Zoom, only underscored that unity, further eliminating the divide between the haves and have-nots and those (most of us) who fall in between.

Yet the crisis was sobering in that it held up a mirror to our true selves, showing what people were made of and who the real unsung heroes of our society are (and they're not the Kardashians, A-list movie stars, or Meghan and Harry). It is the everyday people we took for granted before the pandemic: the healthcare workers, grocery store employees, pharmacy employees, mail carriers, subway conductors, etc. These are the people, the essential workers, who were on the frontlines, putting their lives at risk. They are the ones whom we depended on for our society to be operational when it seemed like so many of us were in suspension.

Perhaps one of the greatest legacies of COVID-19 is that these essential workers may be viewed in a new light in the aftermath while celebrity might be trivialized. If the latter is possible in this celebrity-obsessed culture, let's take a moment and pretend it is. Think of all the news stories of doctors and nurses working themselves to exhaustion in hospitals that didn't have enough ventilators or even beds for infected patients; regular citizens launching campaigns to find more masks and personal protective equipment to donate to hospitals that were in dire need of them; young people offering to shop for and deliver groceries to the elderly or medically fragile; or restaurants forced to shut down during the lockdown providing free meals to healthcare workers who were so insanely busy with attending to the massive, unending overflow of incoming COVID-19 patients they had no time to eat!

Compare these acts of courage, altruism, and charity to the morally grotesque selfishness of billionaires like David Geffen, who said (or gloated?) in an Instagram post that drew heavy backlash, he was riding out the pandemic in a luxurious, fully stocked yacht in the middle of the Caribbean.[2] Featuring a photo of the 454-foot *Rising Sun*, the vessel serving as the venue for his lavish self-isolation, the 77-year-old billionaire wrote, "Isolated in the Grenadines avoiding the virus. I'm hoping everybody is staying safe." The sheer audacity displaced here, as the death toll and number of those infected skyrocketed each day, was as mind-blowing as it was tone-deaf. No surprise that after unleashing a storm of outrage, Geffen reconsidered the optics of the post and made his Instagram private—before he deleted the account.

True, he was not the only one trying to cash in his or her poker chips of rarefied privilege to score wins denied to the riffraff. Think about how early in the crisis when there was a dearth of COVID-19 tests available, how only celebrities and so-called VIPs seemed to have access to them. And while that was going on, average folks with fever and COVID-19 symptoms had limited testing options other than traveling to ad-hoc testing sites at local community colleges where they would wait in long car lines for hours on end, hoping and praying they would make the cutoff point.[3]

But for every celebrity jerk like Geffen, others used their status, money, and resources to do tremendous good. Think of legendary designer Ralph Lauren donating $10 million[4] to the coronavirus relief effort; reality TV star and Skinnygirl founder Bethenny Frankel's tireless efforts[5] via her charity organization BStrong[6] to provide hundreds of thousands of masks to healthcare workers as well as coronavirus kits comprised of items such as hand sanitizers, hydration kits and gloves; and New England Patriots owner Robert Kraft's delivery of 1.2 million protective masks[7] from China to US healthcare workers in need.

Happily, there were dozens more who also joined the philanthropic fold. Sure, cynics might chalk off some of these charitable acts as virtue signaling or attempts to rehabilitate a tarnished reputation after an earlier embarrassing incident, but really—did it matter? Who cares what the true motivators were behind these magnanimous deeds—just as long as they were done. That is the bottom-line and what people should focus on as the crisis fades from memory.

Or, as New York Governor Andrew Cuomo said in a tweet dated April 3, 2020, "I believe our nation will come together because it's the only way to save lives." Or better yet, remember what legendary physicist and Nobel laureate Albert Einstein once said, "Adversity introduces a man to himself."

Yes, maybe I do have a Pollyanna streak, but I agree with the governor and Einstein. Remembering who did their part and who did not will be the major takeaway of this pandemic. At least, I hope.

NOTES

1. CDC Coronavirus Disease 2019, https://www.cdc.gov/coronavirus/2019-ncov/prevent-getting-sick/index.html.

2. Evann Gastaldo, "David Geffen's Self Isolation Yacht Post Not Going Over Well," *Newser*, March 30, 2020, https://www.newser.com/story/288805/david-geffen-hammered-over-self-isolation-yacht-post.html.

3. Christopher Maag, 'What choice do we have?': NJ residents camp out all night in hopes of a coronavirus test," *NorthJersey.com*, March 25, 2020, https://www.northjersey.com/story

/news/columnists/christopher-maag/2020/03/25/coronavirus-nj-sick-residents-wait-all-night-hopes-test/2905859001/?fbclid=IwAR1rgUq0MNIGzq9hxU4O0rOw8HrR4ImHdOcZBWzOZVZuv2D2YL_EChMxqqY.

4. Andrew Nguyen, "Ralph Lauren Donated a Ton of Money for Coronavirus Relief," *The Cut*, March 26, 2020, https://www.thecut.com/2020/03/ralph-lauren-donated-10-million-for-coronavirus-relief.html.

5. Melissa Roberto, "Bethenny Frankel says coronavirus pandemic is 'another level of desperation' as she champions relief efforts," *FoxNews.com*, March 27, 2020, https://www.foxnews.com/entertainment/bethenny-frankel-coronavirus-pandemic-another-level-of-desperation.

6. Bstrong website, https://www.bethenny.com/bstrong-disaster-relief/.

7. Ben Church, "New England Patriots fly 1.2 million protective masks from China after 'challenging' operation," *CNN.com*, April 3, 2020, https://www.cnn.com/2020/04/03/sport/new-england-patriots-masks-robert-kraft-spt-intl/index.html.

⟦ ABOUT THE AUTHOR ⟧ --

IRIS DORBIAN is a professional journalist whose articles and essays have appeared in myriad outlets that include *Forbes, Wall Street Journal, Crain's New York Business, Playbill, Backstage,* and HBO's "Inspiration Room." She is the author of *Sentenced to Shakespeare,* which was published by Sunbury Press/Milford House Press in July 2019.

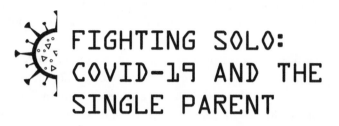

FIGHTING SOLO: COVID-19 AND THE SINGLE PARENT

BY H. A. CALLUM

THE COVID-19 CRISIS has brought about an era of self-imposed isolation many of us have never known. We have become refugees in our own homes, estranged from our modern lifestyles and all its conveniences. While technology has held the fabric of our society close in some social and economic circles, it has failed to prevent many from feeling isolated. Specific populations are at a higher risk of economic damage and loss of personal safeties brought about by this isolation. One such population, often unmentioned in media coverage of the pandemic, is that of single-parent households.

Earlier this year, through a series of dire circumstances, my daughters and I joined the statistics of single-parent households in the United States. According to the U.S. Census Bureau, as of 2016, there were eleven million single-parent households in the U.S.[1] The reasons behind this are many, ranging from the death of a partner/spouse to divorce, abandonment, and, most tragically, domestic violence. The rise of the single-parent household in the U.S. is a specter that continues to haunt American family life and is inapposite to the family values charade bandied about by politicians and religious leaders.

What the COVID-19 crisis has shown is how quickly our accustomed quality of life can decline when modern conveniences, often taken for granted, are stripped away. For any family, dealing with the pandemic can be both emotionally and financially draining. For the working single parent, it beckons a heightened level of crisis in that childcare may be lost, the security provided by school meals is removed, and families on the verge of financial collapse are catapulted over its edge. Furthermore, many single-parent households are also dealing with issues of personal safety now magnified by the crisis. On top of that, there are the routines of daily living that are no longer routine. They have become an almost impossible burden.

For most, the social distancing restrictions in place are no more than a nuisance: long lines at grocery stores, takeout dining in place of restaurant seating, and closed social venues. Many still enjoy the conveniences of modern living. In fact, for some, the pandemic has become an imposed vacation of sorts. For many Americans, their incomes have not been affected—yet. For them, finances remain stable, food is on the table, and "necessary" trips to stores (as loosely as this term has come to be understood) carry on. All the while, the costs of employment for many have been negated, from commuting to childcare.

But single parents do not enjoy these same comforts. We are homebound with our children, unable to bring them on those necessary shopping trips out of fear for their safety and wellbeing. For a single parent, the time to shop is limited, and frequently, nonexistent. When those trips are possible, usually at the most inconvenient times, grocers' shelves may already be bare. For me, the fear of becoming infected with the virus during necessary outings lingers in the back of my mind—if I were to fall ill, who would watch my children? Who would provide their support? While I have been fortunate to have the ability to work from home and care for my daughters, I know of many other single parents who have not been quite as fortunate. I have also had the support of friends and family who have offered to deliver groceries. Sadly, for many single parents, that lifeline does not exist. In this sense, I know I am better off than most.

These fears were realized in our home recently. My youngest daughter has a medical condition that places her at high risk if she were to become infected. In early April, she developed a fever. At once, my already precarious situation suddenly became one of life or death. My daughter's fever came on without warning. All efforts I had made to keep her safe seemed for naught. I watched as my older daughter, a survivor of trauma, entered a level of anxiety that threatened to shatter her already fragile mental state. The fears of the virus appeared to have become a reality despite my best efforts to prevent infection. We were already a statistic, and now we were on the verge of upping the tally of the COVID-19 toll. Nervously, I phoned my pediatrician. I informed friends and family of the potential infection.

There was nothing we could do except wait it out. While her fever broke within twenty-four hours, I spent the next week anxiously hoping that no other symptoms would appear. Serendipity visited us, and her condition improved. At the time this essay went to press, my daughters and I remained symptom-free.

That is not to say that the fears were trivial. The isolation was already there. Our pediatrician was terrific, but her hands were tied. Testing was, and remains, limited. Leaving home would have jeopardized the health of my daughters exponentially, with the risk of us all becoming infected if we were to seek medical treatment. In this time of crisis, those places that typically bring us peace of mind in an emergency—our physicians' offices and medical centers—are vectors of transmission. It was a primal gut feeling knowing that we were indeed on our own. Our survival rested in our own hands. In reality, it rested in my hands alone. That is a dire set of consequences for any parent, and especially when parenting solo.

I knew I couldn't get sick. Two amazing lives were counting on me, as they always had, and now they needed me more than ever to remain strong. I am somewhat lucky to have a certain level of training in dealing with crises from my brief military service that has served my daughters and me well through all of this. I am also a survivor, having overcome Lyme Disease and other personal setbacks. I have the will and means to go on living when others would crumble in the face of adversity. Still, I was tested. My resolve may not have wavered, but the fears and anxiety I felt were significant. Every moment I worried about my daughters' health and my health—not out of concern for myself, but out of concern over their welfare if I were to fall victim to the virus.

To some readers, these circumstances may seem trivial. Some take the luxury of our medical system and first responders for granted. It is those members of society who place all of us at increased risk, and who are risking the lives of the members of the medical community fighting this pandemic under conditions suggestive of battlefield triage scenarios. Life and death have become a matter of who is fit for survival, who can be saved without straining the healthcare system, and likely, who will be able to benefit society once the curve has flattened. Seeing these behaviors suggests to me that priorities have not been adjusted to the new realities of living through a pandemic such as this one.

While we've all been made to readjust our lifestyles to a degree, it has certainly been easier for some than others. In certain ways, it is a mirror of how our society has always operated. But there is a much darker side to the plight of single-parent households in the U.S. Many single parents and their children are refugees. They have escaped violence and abuse. Life has already been a challenge, and now it is even more daunting. The fact remains that sheltering in place may have dire consequences for parents and their children struggling to flee a hostile home environment. With nowhere else to go, some remain in situations that pose imminent physical threats. If they have managed to escape, access to the court system for child support and other safety nets may have been delayed. While the criminal justice system remains intact, the fact is that single parents and their children continue to be at high risk from physical harm in these situations. The diminishment of economic and social safeguards only further jeopardizes these vulnerable members of society.

My daughters and I endured such a situation. We were fortunate to have ended it and to have become stable in our home before the quarantine measures were imposed. Had they been enacted sooner, that may not have been the case, and our home life would not be the sanctuary it has become. For us, the timing was impeccable. Still, I am quick to remember that many were not quite as lucky. These are the families forgotten amidst the pandemic. They continue to suffer in silence.

I remain hopeful that all is not grim. What the COVID-19 crisis has shown is that our society can change. Working from home for all families can be viable after this crisis has passed. Employers may come to recognize that productivity has not suffered and that employees are happier. Children spend more time at home. The financial burdens faced by all working families may ease somewhat. We may remain far from realizing this potential, but in the end, it is an ideal that is not out of reach. We are now living it under dire circumstances. Without the looming anxiety of a global pandemic, perhaps those with the power to enact change will do so and will make the ideal of the American family a truth and not an unobtainable fiction.

My daughters and I are seeing the benefits of this in our own lives. The rigors of juggling work, child-raising, and maintaining a home are not easy. However, as our situation has changed, the home has once again become a place of peace and healing. We remain a busy, modern family who has been given the benefit of slowing down. We enjoy our time alone. Days at the playground have been replaced with walks and bike rides. We cook meals together and enjoy them at the table as a family. We are a family again because we fled a dangerous situation, and because COVID-19 has allowed us to be together without interruption. While the pandemic has caused concern, and I've noted that anxiety in my daughters, I am present to give them comfort and the age-appropriate knowledge to help relax their fears. Better yet, we have this time to heal from the pain of a not-so-distant past and restore our family. What the COVID-19 crisis has given us is the time to reflect on what matters most. It is, and always will be, the people we hold closest to us.

I've always held my daughters close. Unconditional love is that love between a parent and a child, and there is a trove of clichéd lines about this bond. However, they all fall short. We are all parents to the children of this world. To quote Toni Morrison, "When a kid walks in a room, your child or anybody else's child, does your face light up? That's what they're looking for." Wherever you are, be that light to the face of a child, especially now. In action, love is advanced. In love, there is hope.

Because, in the end, love always wins.

NOTE

1. "The Majority of Children Live with Two Parents, Census Bureau Reports," United States Census Bureau, November 17, 2016, https://www.census.gov/newsroom/press-releases/2016/cb16 -192.html.

⟦ ABOUT THE AUTHOR ⟧

H. A. CALLUM is a writer and poet from the Philadelphia suburbs and holds a Bachelor of Arts in English (summa cum laude) from the Pennsylvania State University. He's a father first and spends his time away from the writing desk chasing unicorns with his daughters. Mr. Callum's poetry and fiction have appeared in local and national literary journals. His debut literary novel, *Whispers in the Alders*, was published by Brown Posey Press in 2018.

LEFT BEHIND

BY CATHERINE JORDAN

MY KIDS WERE potentially exposed to COVID-19. They were told to stay home and self-isolate for 14 days. No biggie. They were comfortably isolated with their computers and their cell phones. Online video games, podcasts, Zoom, streaming, social media, and Tik Tok helped tick away the minutes of the day and the boredom.

Ask an elder about Tik Tok.

"Tick . . . What?"

Then try explaining Tik Tok's mission: to capture and present the world's creativity, knowledge, and precious life moments. Real people, spontaneous short-form videos.

Technology makes life fun, interesting, and easier, but only if you know how to use it. My daughter attended a Zoom birthday party. The happy celebrant opened presents for all those watching, and even cut his cake to a chorus of "oos" and "ahhs." As a family, we've been sharing pictures of our dinner and dessert recipes. You know, the finished product in all its glory, right before it gets wolfed down. We've been forwarding online articles and taking silly quizzes with song challenges.

My kids never knew life without a personal computer. They learned how to use their phones and Nintendo at an early age, and on their own. I didn't know how to use them and didn't want to learn, nor did I have the patience. But then, smartphones and apps came along. So did Amazon and home shopping. My high school reunion was organized around Facebook with invites and save the date and who was attending. Then I published a book and needed to learn how to market myself online. So, I learned.

Sure, my mom could use a washing machine and an ATM, but technology changes fast, and rather than admit defeat, she just wouldn't bother trying. She refused to get a smartphone. I told her the grandkids text but won't pick up the phone to reach out and touch someone. That's okay, she said, because since kids nowadays talk with a rapid-fire bullet spray of words, it's almost like listening to another language. Smartphones and Facebook, I told her, would allow her to listen to her grandkids with subtitles, and see their faces. "I like my flip phone," she said.

When my mom died a few years ago, I found it necessary for my dad and me to communicate almost daily, but I live over an hour away. So, I insisted he upgrade from a flip phone to a smartphone. Then I introduced him to social media. His grandkids helped him download apps. He eventually met his new partner on a dating site. But my dad's the exception. This article isn't about my parents. Rather, it's about the willingness of older adults to embrace technology.

Marketers agree that elders have the potential to be the fastest-growing technology market. Joseph F. Coughlin wrote in his *Barron's* article, "It's the mother of all untapped markets: the world's 65-plus population. Already at a historical high of over 600 million people, it's projected to hit a full billion by 2030, and 1.6 billion by 2050."

So why hasn't it happened yet?

Marketers are savvy, and they've already successfully marketed newer technologies by appealing to older adult's fear of life-threatening situations, like being alone, falls, or other health-related issues like a stroke or heart attack. This demographic, however, also needs technology that provides convenience, independence, and social connectivity. And there are lots of things available, like Joy For All Companion Pets robotic cats and dogs. In fact, I just had this discussion the other day with an older friend. I'd love a cat that doesn't scratch my furniture, won't cost a fortune in vet bills, or need to have the litter box emptied. This friend had no idea the technology and the product already exist. He has a laptop. He just doesn't use it.

In my opinion, the digital divide between older and younger can be attributed to three things: frustration, ignorance, and security concerns particularly in financial matters. Even though screen time has increased for the over-65 population, and so has familiarity with the existence of technology in general, challenges persist.

Dr. Bran Knowles and Professor Vicki Hanson, in their paper "The Wisdom of Older Technology (non) Users," call blaming age for non-use of technology, "playing the age card." Doctor Knowles goes on to say that, "Doing so allows older adults a privilege not available to most working-age adults to take personal stands against the aspects of technology they find worrying, threatening, or just plain annoying." In other words, older adults are perfectly capable; they just don't want to. Efficiency clearly does not motivate them to use technology. But will necessity?

Technology can ease the difficulties of this pandemic era. Again, only if you know how to use it. I consider it essential for the younger generation to help familiarize the older with technology. Although a large portion of elders refused to hop on the tech-train by "playing the age card," they have a lot of catching up to do to avoid being left behind.

I work with elders who live in an apartment home geared towards their needs. The apartment building has a community store, a small beauty shop, a public dining room, a compact library, and an activity room. Considering the proximity for all these conveniences, this age-in-place standard of living has worked against them. You've read the news. You know the virus is culling this age group.

Tape strips on the walls show the six-feet social distance that must be kept from friends, neighbors, and even the aides. The six-feet social distance standard has been troublesome, to say the least. Groups of ten or less has also been an issue. You can't blame aides who have chosen to stay at home and protect themselves. Same with the housecleaners who used to wipe their toilet seats and disinfect their sinks.

COVID-19 isn't the only concern for older adults. Trust me; they need to interact with the outside world. I've seen the effect depression has on them. It is setting in quickly with their isolation. They are truly alone. They are scared. They are filled with anxiety. So, you might be thinking, why don't they talk to someone, get some exercise, obtain an anti-anxiety prescription? Well, that answer might seem easy, but COVID-19 has complicated it.

If they want to talk, that involves socializing in places like coffee shops and fast-food chains. My elderly friends particularly like McDonald's, where no one is waiting to be seated, no waitstaff stands in the wings for a tip, and they can sit and drink coffee all morning long without being disturbed.

Exercise? Mall walking provides flat terrain, a quick seat if winded, and a water fountain if thirsty. Treadmills and bikes at the local gym are easy to use, quite practical and under an air-conditioned roof.

Doctor visits? Hospital and medical visits for everyday aches and irritations are essential, and another means of socialization. I hear them complain, but I think they like having a reason to go for a drive and talk to the friendly staff. They often see a friend or an acquaintance there as well.

But now the governor has ordered all nonessential businesses to close. Store, mall, theater, bank lobby, and restaurant closures have had a devastating impact on elder lifestyle. In some states, the family isn't allowed to visit their parents because of the disease and its contagion. McDonald's is either the drive-thru or Grubhub. The mall-walk or the gym is only accessible via YouTube. Those doctor visits? My doctor once told me she highly recommended I get my entire family into the system where we can be accessed, diagnosed, prescribed medication, and track our healthcare online; web visits were the future. They are now the present.

A gentleman approached me last week with several checks he needed to deposit. But the bank lobbies are closed. He's confined to a wheelchair, and I can't get him into my car. He doesn't trust anyone with his ATM card or his PIN. So, the checks remain in his pocket.

Taxes? The van visit to H&R Block has been canceled. H&R Block is online, you say. Turbo Tax is a game-changer, you say. Ah, but the tax filing date has been extended to July 15th. "I'll go by then," they say.

As far as the news is concerned, the television is their preferred source for information. It's their connection to humankind. But they can barely process one headline on CNN or Fox before it's replaced with a new headline. Who can trust the media when they use nebulous words, like might, would, or could? Social media, however, has positive spaces with memes, jokes, and "good news only" feeds. A common response: "Nope—not doin' it." Still, the older adults sit back and wait for the world to return to normal.

Will the world go back to life-as-usual? I haven't the heart to tell my elder friends that we've been thrust into a new normal. Life has changed forever.

Alvin Toffler's book, *Future Shock*, first published in 1970, is about what happens to people overwhelmed by change. He says that the death of permanence, increase in life's pace, and transience are consequences of change. Technology dependence is also a consequence. Maybe the older generation thought they'd never need those skills, or that its know-how would fall upon the next generation. But no one expected a pandemic, and no one predicted our dependence on the Internet for life's necessities, like exercise, doctor visits, and socialization. My kids have coped just fine. So have I. But older people crave facetime; unfortunately, to get it, it's going to be on a screen. COVID-19 is forcing those "playing the age card" to "fold."

⟦ ABOUT THE AUTHOR ⟧ --

CATHERINE JORDAN is an avid writer of short stories, articles, and novels who also leads writers' groups. She has been a judge for the Bram Stoker and ITW Young Adult Awards. In her spare time, she volunteers with the elderly. Catherine lives in Pennsylvania with her husband and five children.

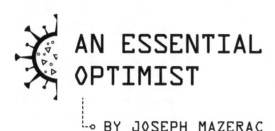

AN ESSENTIAL OPTIMIST

BY JOSEPH MAZERAC

TOMORROW, I'LL BE heading out the door at 6:30 A.M., like nothing unusual is happening. The only indications otherwise will be the incredible lack of traffic and a bottle of hand sanitizer in my cupholder. Apparently, I'm "essential personnel."

For those of you reading this in the future, the United States is on various levels of lockdown. Across America, governors are issuing shelter-in-place orders. I'm a Floridian, but work has me finishing a project in North Carolina.

The virus is coming. In fact, it's already here. It's in Florida, too, with deaths recorded in my county. I'm still at the stage where all the closed businesses seem more real than the actual sickness, but that will change soon. Over the coming weeks, people will get sick by the hundreds of thousands—or millions—the healthcare system will struggle to care for them all, and deaths will multiply. At this point, that grim prognosis seems unavoidable. Yet, while I acknowledge the unfolding disaster, I'm an optimist at heart.

Considering everything we are facing, one could wonder what on earth there is to be optimistic about. It's not as if we can wash our hands fifty times a day, agree to cough into our elbows, and click our heels together three times, and the virus will magically poof out of existence. It's not like that at all. But that doesn't mean we're entirely without hope.

I try to picture the world a year from now. And what about in two years, will our lives look any different than they did six months ago? And that's the thing. They will.

Let me look into my crystal ball and gaze into its glimmer. The haziness of the present gives way, and the near future is uncertain, but beyond I see a light.

As soon as regular folks can shake hands again, and the kids go back to school, and we can go to church, or the ball game, or gas stations without wishing we had level D Hazmat suits, the worst will be behind us. I know for some, that will be hard to hear. For those who've lost someone during the pandemic, there's no replacing a loved one. Time saws off the past, and there's no getting it back. Wounded survivors will struggle with a kind of isolation that lasts longer than a government-mandated quarantine. Healing will be painful and slow. Likely, they'll have to rely on others in ways they never did before. But regardless of past and present suffering, the world will move on in a way that's not entirely heartbreaking.

People will make new bonds with family and friends. We'll find new jobs, and new children will come into the world, filling us with brand-new hopes and worries. Little ones are running around even now who will remember the year they had school at home on their computers but will forget the virus that caused the situation. Those kids will have dreams that have nothing to do with COVID-19. And so will we. In two short years, when Virgin Galactic is sending billionaires into space at $300,000 a seat, and Tesla fanboys are cruising the boulevards in their Cybertrucks, this time of crisis will feel like a bad dream.

The train of life will chug on down the rails long after this pandemic is over. There isn't anything particularly surprising about that. But I submit to you; we are presented with a rare opportunity. After experiencing the stress and isolation, I ask, why not come out of our quarantines a little happier to see our neighbors? Why not be a little more courteous, more open, and more helpful to our communities? Because here is the truth that too often remains unrecognized, we actually need each other. You need other people. Me, too. It's okay.

If the virus can teach us anything, it should be something akin to the butterfly effect. Even our smallest choices affect others, sometimes in oversized ways. This isn't a new idea, and there's no getting around it. A person encounters a bat virus halfway around the world, and next thing you know, the entire population is infected. With the pandemic, the principle is playing out in front of the whole world in the most terrible way imaginable. But that same principle is busy every day, a million times a day, in exchanges both good and bad. Every interaction sends ripples out across humanity like waves over the surface of a pond. How the waves affect us is too complex to understand. Sometimes they combine to amplify, and other times they cancel each other out, but they always do something.

You can divide groups of people as small or as large as you like—family, neighborhood, city, state, nation, world—and it all amounts to the same. One person helps or hurts someone else, and on and on the ripples go. It's always worked this way, backward through history and forward into the future, the present riding the wave.

If our visions were grand enough, we'd see we're not just a solitary planet, either. The universe is the pool in which we swim. And don't get me started on the complexity of time, how we're all connected in ways unfathomable to the human imagination. This virus puts that into perspective.

If the pandemic is still going when you read this, here's my advice—besides the typical stuff about washing your hands and keeping your distance. If you're on lockdown, make the most of it. Whoever you're sheltered with is your temporary micro-community.

When I get home, I intend to revel in my family. I'll enjoy a little home cooking, make a few meals myself, and give my wife a break for a change. I'll take my dog out in the backyard, let him sniff around and pee on things while I drink my morning coffee and talk to God. That sounds nice.

I want to make some good memories, too—do something really nutty like letting my kids have a peanut-butter-smeared wrestling match in the garage. I know what you're thinking, *the mess!* But can you imagine how glorious? They'd remember it for decades.

It shouldn't take the threat of death to force my family together. My life gets too busy, and I splash through my days without thinking of all the waves I'm making. Where are all those ripples going? Do you ever wonder about that? What are the effects on the other side of the pond?

I plead with you to remember the lesson of the virus and be careful with what you are doing. This lesson is for me as much as anybody. I need to be more generous. That's resonating with me. And I need to find a way to help in this situation because that's the guy I want to be. I have one idea. A small one. I think there's a place I can get some respirators. It might only be a box or two, but that's something. Little waves count.

And, God help me, when all this is over, I'm finally going to invite Jay and his wife to the house for dinner.

Much love from North Carolina, and, to my family, I should be home soon.

〔 ABOUT THE AUTHOR 〕 --

JOSEPH MAZERAC worked as essential personnel on a government project during the time of the COVID-19 crisis. He is also the author of *Into the Attic of the World* and host of the Blue Deck Podcast.

PUBLIC HEALTH, CIVIL LIBERTIES, AND LIFE AFTER THE PANDEMIC

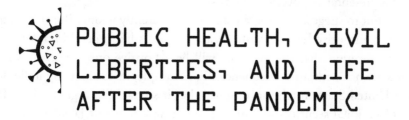

⌐o BY SCOTT ZUCKERMAN, M. D.

THE WORLD HAS changed. It has changed abruptly, dramatically, and with little warning, and it is probably going to stay changed in ways we can hardly imagine. Unquestionably, the field of medicine will never be the same. Some of the transformations that occur as a result of the coronavirus pandemic could be for the betterment of public health, while some will be to its detriment. Depending on one's vantage point, the distinction between help and hindrance may be a shade of gray. Since the situation in which we find ourselves is unprecedented during human history, any speculation about how the future will look is based on mere guesswork, rather than on scientific evidence or factual data. The collective populace may have the opportunity to shape some outcomes, while other consequences will be inescapable. In the words of the late Joe Strummer, "The future is unwritten."

In 1755, Benjamin Franklin wrote, "Those who would give up essential liberty, to purchase a little temporary safety, deserve neither liberty nor safety." To slow the spread of coronavirus, civil liberties have been broadly curtailed to a degree never seen in the United States. Gatherings—whether for religious or social purposes—have been restricted. Businesses have been forced to close, and for some, those closures may prove permanent. Individuals have been stopped and questioned for screening at state borders. Access to national and state parks has been denied. Curfews have been imposed. Perhaps these measures were indeed necessary to limit the transmission of the disease and thereby reduce the ultimate number of casualties. Perhaps. But most of these decisions were made without the usually requisite objective proof of their value and the approval of Congress or even local representative governing bodies.

This is not to suggest that these plans were inherently wrong. But it is a slippery slope to authorize set rules only because it seems like a good idea, without adequate verification that the outcome will be a positive one, especially when those rules are not without consequences. For example, in 1942, many individuals in the United States might have agreed that it seemed like a good idea—for the sake of national security—to confine American citizens of Japanese descent in isolated camps, denying those individuals their civil rights. But today, we can look back on that decision and accurately describe it as one of the most egregious mistakes of the twentieth century. I am in no way suggesting that the restrictions pertaining to the control of the coronavirus are as pernicious as the internment of over one hundred thousand innocent Japanese-Americans; to do so would be demeaning to their experience and blind to the overt racism that prevailed during that dark chapter. But in a country that has historically valued liberty over all other considerations ("Give me liberty or give me death!"), it has been interesting to witness the widespread acceptance of these drastic limitations, with little—if any—protest or rebellion.

So how does this pertain to the field of medicine? There have been many instances when the objective of improving the overall health of the population has come in direct conflict with the inclination to preserve liberty—however it is defined—no matter what the cost. Often, the pursuit of liberty has trumped the ambition of improving the well-being of the community. One very recent—and highly publicized—example of this is the debate over vaccinations. The development of vaccines is one of the greatest achievements in the history of medicine. Anyone who would argue against this statement needs to be educated regarding infectious diseases such as polio, diphtheria, and smallpox, which inflicted and killed millions of people before effective vaccines were developed.

The facts are, however, that no vaccine is one hundred percent effective, and no vaccine is without (rare) adverse side effects. To eliminate a disease, therefore, all members of the population must receive the vaccine, creating what is referred to as "herd immunity." The eradication of smallpox from the world population in the 1970s is a perfect illustration of how universal vaccination can succeed. Today, medical professionals are in direct conflict with so-called "anti-vaxxers," who refuse to vaccinate their children because of religious reasons, or because they've been coerced by a fraudulent study—conducted by a physician who has since been discredited—that erroneously linked measles, mumps, rubella (MMR) vaccine to autism. And for the most part, these misguided, selfish individuals have been allowed the liberty to refrain from vaccinating their children, thereby endangering the health of all persons with whom they come in contact. The result has been a resurgence in the incidence of measles—which had been virtually eliminated from the United States by 1980. The virus that causes measles, while far less deadly than the coronavirus, is known to be considerably more contagious. According to the World Health Organization, there were over 140,000 deaths from measles globally in 2018.

So now that a precedent has been established during the coronavirus pandemic, will the recommendations of medical scientists consistently override certain aspects of "freedom of religion" to preserve the health of the general population? It seems likely that if an effective, safe vaccine against coronavirus is developed, the government will mandate that every eligible individual receives it. Time will tell. From my perspective, as a pediatrician, this would be a good outcome, not just for this disease, but for all infectious diseases, past and present.

Our understanding of the specific epidemiology of COVID-19 might give rise to some positive changes as well. It would seem, at least given the available data so far, that individuals with certain chronic conditions who become infected with coronavirus are at far higher risk for developing severe symptoms and dying. The list includes diabetes, hypertension, cardiovascular disease, and chronic pulmonary disease. Will the dramatic increase in mortality due to coronavirus in association with these mostly preventable conditions finally convince the general public to adopt lifestyle changes that are clearly in their best interest? Eat less and exercise more? Eat more fruits and vegetables—and real food in general—instead of high-fat, high-carbohydrate processed food whose ingredients are unrecognizable? Give up smoking? There is some recent evidence that long-term exposure to airborne pollutants also increases the risk of an adverse outcome from COVID-19. So, will that association prompt some aggressive momentum toward cleaning the air which we breathe?

One would hope that everyone will recognize their responsibilities and take ownership of their health and well-being. While that has not usually proven to be the case, past attempts to legislate issues such as obesity and diabetes—a prime example being the short-lived New York City ban on jumbo sodas in 2012—have proven to be ill-conceived and poorly received. Of course, the battle against the use of tobacco has been much more effective, with various forms of legislation contributing to a fifty percent reduction in cigarette smoking over the past half-century. One glaring difference between these two issues—and this pertains to the vaccine discussion as well—is that smoking a cigarette has a substantial effect on those around you, while that is not necessarily so with regard to drinking a one-liter cup of Coca-Cola (unless you happen to be sitting next to that individual on an airplane.)

The elderly seem to be at risk for more severe coronavirus sequelae than younger individuals. Throughout the world, there have been tragic instances of the infection spreading through nursing homes and causing devastation not only to the inhabitants but also to the staff. As the youngest Baby Boomers in the United States are now turning sixty, and the population grows older with each passing year, will this pandemic result in a change in how our society treats older folks? Will we return to the old way of caring for our elders at home rather than institutionalizing them? For those who reside in such facilities out of necessity, will health insurance finally cover the associated expenses, raising the quality of care in the process? Will appropriate value finally be given to the most endur-ing—and often the most vulnerable—members of our society?

I know I have posed more questions than I have provided answers. But as much as I would like to be optimistic about mankind's response to this situation, my pessimistic nature—cemented in place by my life-long observation of human behavior—makes me unsure that people will ever collectively choose to do the right thing. After all, in 2020, faced with a respiratory virus that causes respiratory symptoms, the primary motivation of the population at large seems to have become an irrational quest to stockpile toilet paper.

[ABOUT THE AUTHOR] ---

DR. SCOTT ZUCKERMAN has been practicing medicine for over thirty years. He has been board-certified in pediatrics, pediatric emergency medicine, and medical acupuncture. His high school English teacher, Frank McCourt–who would later win a Pulitzer Prize for his memoir, *Angela's Ashes*–inscribed in his yearbook, "You have displayed the writer's gift. Cultivate it." Forty years later, Zuckerman heeded McCourt's advice. His first book, *Dreams of My Comrades*, was awarded first place in the nonfiction category of the 2015 Utah Original Writing Competition, and was published in 2017 by Sunbury Press.

MEDICINE IN THE POST-
CORONAPOCALYPSE ERA

⌐o BY SCOTT ZUCKERMAN, M. D.

THE CORONAVIRUS PANDEMIC has profoundly reshaped the way we connect with one another. Its effects are likely to continue long after the threat of this particular infection has subsided. The relationships that exist between doctors and patients will never be the same. But the seeds of change were planted decades ago, they were nourished by the greed of a few and the apathy of many, and now those seeds are about to bloom into mature, noxious, invasive weeds.

The concept of the doctor-patient relationship might seem charming and archaic today, but it wasn't so long ago that doctors and patients did indeed have relationships. I finished medical school in 1985, and I remember it well. I chose a career in pediatrics, and the typical pattern was to see a baby in the nursery soon after they were born, then guide the parents through each step of infancy and later childhood and adolescence, navigating the mundane tasks of vaccination alongside the more significant challenges of illness and injury. There were so many kids I had the pleasure to treat as they grew from newborns into teenagers. And I imagined myself continuing to attend to them, maybe even getting invited to a wedding or two, and then taking care of their kids, too.

Then in the 1990s, the insurance companies interdigitated themselves between the patients and their doctors. The bean-counters and number-crunchers started to decide which patients could see which doctors, what each doctor could do, how long each visit should be, and how much each doctor should get paid for each encounter. And the greed of the actuaries, compounded by the apathy of the doctors, allowed it to happen. So, the inmates were running the asylum—but they weren't running it well—and they were siphoning a lot of money right out of the system. So just to maintain their standard of living, physicians had to see more patients every hour, more patients every day, more patients every week. And patients were forced to change doctors every time their employer changed insurance plans. I can attest to this firsthand: In 1995, I saw twenty percent more patients every day, but my income was decreased by twenty percent compared to the previous year. And the daily turnover of patients in my practice was even more dramatic. So much for those wedding invitations. The seeds of change were planted.

In the 2000s, the fertilizer that was added to this tragic garden came in the form of electronic medical records—a great concept that was ruined by avarice and stupidity. The systems, which should have been designed by physicians to streamline and standardize communication, were instead developed by computer geeks, with the primary purpose of maximizing the capacity of the insurance companies to collect money. Having spent many nights caring for patients in the emergency room, I had been hopeful for an accurate electronic record that could be checked no matter where the patient might be. A six-year-old with a fever, visiting New Jersey from North Dakota, whose mother only speaks Swedish, shows up at midnight? No problem: access the kid's medical record and immediately know their entire history, including immunizations and allergies. Such a system would be invaluable. But rather than being useful, the systems are bulky, confusing, time-consuming, and illogical, and even worse, the multitude of systems on the market have no way of communicating with each other. So that proverbial kid in my hypothetical ER? I have a better chance of instantaneously learning Swedish than of gathering any useful information from the electronic medical records—if I can even access them at all.

The result has been a further deterioration of each encounter with each patient—already abbreviated out of necessity—now spent mostly clicking away at a keyboard rather than making eye-contact or any sort of meaningful connection with the patient.

And now it's 2020. And the coronavirus pandemic—and accompanying media-fueled hysteria—has seized the world and has its firmest grasp on the throat of the medical community. To avoid unnecessary contact and exposure, patients are being told to stay home unless they need care urgently. Countless visits are being conducted remotely via telemedicine or telephone. And it won't take long before that becomes the new standard, long after the virus has run its belligerent course. And the insurance companies will decide how much (if at all) doctors should be paid for those encounters. And the electronic medical records will be updated to reflect the new standard of care and maximize corporate profits. And the every-diminishing contact with the patient will have been whittled away to the smallest possible remnant of what it once was.

Hippocrates is credited with saying, "It has often appeared, while I have been soothing my patients, as if there was a singular property in my hands to pull and draw away from the affected parts aches and diverse impurities, by laying my hand upon the place. Thus, it is known to some of the learned that health may be implanted in the sick by certain gestures, and by contact . . ."

A bit of hyperbole? Perhaps. But there's more than a grain of truth there, as well. I'm pretty sure Hippocrates could not have envisioned—and wouldn't be too pleased with—the current and future state of the relationship between a physician and his or her patient. But in all fairness, he wasn't omniscient, either. It wasn't until many centuries after Hippocrates that Ignaz Semmelweis finally convinced all of us that it might be a good idea to wash your hands in between performing autopsies and examining patients, which is a good idea, by the way.

To be honest, it's not just in the world of medicine that human interaction is dwindling. People would rather text than chat over coffee, or maybe they'd prefer to be texting with one person while they're sitting and having coffee with another. People would rather stream music or a film than go to a concert or the movies. They'd prefer watching a ballgame at home in high definition on their big-screen television instead of going to the arena or the stadium. Kids would choose to play a video game on the sofa, over shooting some hoops with their friends. So really, society has been preparing for social distancing for quite some time now; the pandemic has merely—albeit dramatically—accelerated the process.

⟦ ABOUT THE AUTHOR ⟧ --

DR. SCOTT ZUCKERMAN has been practicing medicine for over thirty years. He has been board-certified in pediatrics, pediatric emergency medicine, and medical acupuncture. His high school English teacher, Frank McCourt—who would later win a Pulitzer Prize for his memoir, *Angela's Ashes*—inscribed in his yearbook, "You have displayed the writer's gift. Cultivate it." Forty years later, Zuckerman heeded McCourt's advice. His first book, *Dreams of My Comrades*, was awarded first place in the nonfiction category of the 2015 Utah Original Writing Competition, and was published in 2017 by Sunbury Press.

THE LOOMING HEALTH INSURANCE PROBLEM

BY WILL DELAVAN

WRITING ABOUT THE future is fun; by the time the future gets here, most people have forgotten what you wrote, and if you are lucky enough to have been right, you are an instant visionary, unquestioned. As an economist, I am often asked to predict what is going to happen to the price of some widget or some whatchamacallit next year. I usually defer as I am not a wizard, but the pandemic has brought out my curious side since I am teaching Health Economics right now and there is no downside, only the small chance of being a visionary, I could not resist.

The pandemic has exposed the ugly underbelly[1] of the American health care system leading some to dream that the pandemic will awaken policymakers inducing them to quickly adopt a system of universal health care, a single-payer system, or some combination of the two—something pretty much every developed nation in this world has. Will the dream come true? "Never," bellows the new visionary. We will never tackle the thorniest, gnarliest, most unsettling problem with our system—the fact that access to quality health care is income-based and uneven. When we discuss health care reform, we avoid the prime moral question of social justice and instead fight over the technical details. I do not believe even something as stark and momentous as a global pandemic can change the conversation since the narrative of health care reform is, to date, a false one. A meaningful discussion has never genuinely begun because it has been derailed or usurped by a political movement to treat health care as a free competitive market. Real change can only occur if the narrative starts with an honest appraisal of both the nature of what health care is and, more importantly, social ethics. That is, we must answer the question that health economist Uwe Reinhardt always led off with "To what extent should rich members of society be made to be their poor brothers' and sisters' keepers in health care?"[2] Indeed.

The idea that this pandemic may move us to a more equitable system means that we must address Reinhardt's question of distributive social justice first. This is not going to happen. Everyone knows the stats, although many would like to fantasize about American exceptionalism in health care. The statistics do not change much. Forty million uninsured, now only twenty million due to the mild success of the much-beleaguered Patient Protection Affordable Care Act (ACA), an underdog to begin with, with lukewarm support, that was pushed through like a cadaver at *Weekend at Bernie's*. At the top end, we have some of the best clinical results and technology money can, will, and does buy. On the other side of the ledger, health care in the U.S. is twice as expensive as it is in Europe, and the rate of growth in health care spending exceeds the rate of inflation. And the outcomes are not superior to what other health systems deliver. We pay twice as much as other countries do for the same services and we have very uneven access to them. Our infant mortality rate is comparable to rates in the third world.[3,4] Quite exceptional.

Politicians have been putzing around with technical solutions and getting nowhere for decades; always and everywhere kabuki, artifice, and symbolic gestures. Some of the acts have been genuine, most not. Policymakers have been posing at reform since at least the sixties when Medicare was born. Finally, in 2010 came the Patient Protection and Affordable Care Act. The act was much maligned, but it did something to change the debate. It was a long and sloppy attempt at health care reform, which really meant health insurance reform. If health insurance could be improved, the logic goes, then health care and health outcomes will be improved. If everyone were insured, we would no longer have to bear the burden of uncompensated care. Millions would take advantage of preventative care, or so it was thought, and this would lead to a decrease in emergency room visits. Americans will have universal access to quality health care, no matter how much money you have. But they do not, and the system is broken.

Is it possible that the COVID-19 pandemic and our failings to deal with it will be an event that transforms our health system into the ideal single-payer system with affordable universal care? Can this horrible pandemic awaken us to come to our collective senses and turn a complex byzantine caste system of health care into the world's model? Will American exceptionalism again reveal itself with glory? Where the rest of the world had failed, will we invent a new hero and triumph over viral foes?

One would think that this would indeed be the call for ultimate action. Consider the system a total wreck, collect the insurance, and get a new one. Not so fast. The biggest problem we have from a policy standpoint is that we do not understand or have gotten away from the ability to distinguish between private and public goods. So badly do we misunderstand what health care and health insurance are that we scoff at the idea that everyone be mandated to have insurance—as if health insurance is the same as broccoli.[5] If you don't like broccoli, you don't have to buy it! And so, it should be with health insurance and public health—it should be treated as a private good in a competitive market. Let the market do the work.

The market as an institution, and especially the idea of an unfettered market where no one is forced to purchase anything, is a powerful narrative, but it is a complex concept that has been misunderstood. Broccoli is different from health, health care, and health insurance. One way of distinguishing goods is by looking at two characteristics: rivalry and excludability. Broccoli is a private good that is both rival and excludable. If I eat this piece of broccoli, you cannot eat the same piece of broccoli—it is rival. It is also excludable—I cannot have the broccoli for free, I must pay someone for the broccoli. Broccoli is a pure private good—it is rival and excludable. Markets work very well with pure private goods; these are the markets we rightfully celebrate.

Contrast this idea of a pure private good with a pure public good, one that is non-rival and non-excludable. Since I mentioned American exceptionalism earlier, let us talk about national defense. National defense is non-rival. If I am defended, it does not reduce the amount of protection my neighbors receive. Also, once the national defense is deployed or produced, I benefit from it even if I do not pay for it. Or to make me sound like a good citizen, if I were to produce another child somehow, I would not have to pay more for national defense. It is non-excludable. My extra child can ride free.

The problem with treating health care and health insurance in market terms as private goods is that it does not apply. Private goods markets work well when there are many buyers and sellers, perfect information, no external costs (or benefits), well-defined property rights, and low transaction costs. They do not work when any of these conditions are absent. Even markets for private goods that are in so-called competitive markets do not always work well. Witness now the problem with masks. We have everything but masks, and that is the weakest link. We do not make masks in the U.S. The lack of a decent mask means that other markets fail as well. Without masks, doctors and nurses cannot function.

Most things we value have elements of rivalry and excludability—they are neither pure public nor pure private goods. Health, health care, and health insurance fall in this category. The demand for health insurance is what economists call a derived demand; it is derived from the demand for health care, which is derived from our primary demand for health.

So, when we talk about health insurance, what we are talking about is health. One thing that broccoli has that health does not is some degree of certainty. We typically know how we like or do not like our broccoli, and we can easily measure how much broccoli we have and how much it costs. We often do not know what good or ill health will befall us. We often do not know what is wrong when something feels wrong, or even what makes us feel right. When we go to the doctor, if we can afford it, we may know our symptoms and conditions but are unable to describe them to a doctor. The doctor may not know for certain what is up with their patient and must test and prod and use their experience to make an educated guess. In most cases, the doctor will know—and if you are one of the lucky ones who can use your employer-based insurance to cover some or all of her cost—which incidentally is hard to know as well—then you are truly fortunate and potentially cured. We are uncertain both about the diagnosis, the eventual outcomes, and about prices. Imagine buying broccoli without knowing the price of broccoli before you purchase it? Buying health care is like going into a supermarket blindfolded with a list from a stranger and asked to shop effectively.

The other thing that broccoli lacks that health has in abundance, and this is essential to understanding the public nature of health, is the contagion factor. Looking up a couple of paragraphs—I said that public goods are non-excludable. I cannot catch "the broccolis" from you, but I, as sure as sugar is sweet, can catch COVID-19 from you or anyone, or someone else. Its non-excludable, non-rival, non-partial, and non-discriminatory.

Because health is fraught with uncertainty and because many health conditions may be contagious, we need to think about health, health care, and health insurance in a much more nuanced way than how we think about vegetables and other private goods. A mandate to have health insurance or some other mechanism to ensure everyone is insured, provides benefits to society, recognizes the public and social nature of inhabiting these bodies of ours, and reflects our values. While it is theoretically possible not to encounter other humans, it is not theoretically possible to live forever in these aging bodies. Eventually, we die. As we age, we typically have more health concerns. Like automobiles, the human body fails with age; parts wear out at varying rates and at the most unexpected times, independent of the work we do. We depreciate. We can get cancer or some other severe disease even when we are clean-living, loving, good-neighbor types. There is a great deal of randomness in health outcomes even with proper care, we all eventually die. The combination of uncertainty, contagion, and aging means that public health and health insurance are not private goods. Policy solutions that may work in private markets do not work well with public goods.

Yet some policymakers continue to treat health insurance and health care as pure private goods. Paul Ryan's bill, H.R.1628—American Health Care Act of 2017[6], did exactly this. We were, and I think still are, moving as fast as we can from the idea of universal care towards broccoli-care. Ever since Medicare began to serve both private and social wellbeing, politicians have, perhaps inadvertently, created a caste system for health care where it is rationed by income. A system birthed and nurtured by lobbyists from the medical and insurance industries means that most policy debates were and remain amoral technical charades, thinly veiled attempts to dupe voters. For those who genuinely sought and seek a new model, a mix of private and public insurance, and universal coverage, policy-makers settled for the compromise Patient Protection and Affordable Care Act (PPACA), known also as The Affordable Care Act (ACA) for short.

The ACA offered what the conservative Heritage Foundation offered thirty years earlier, and Mitt Romney in Massachusetts had delivered ten years earlier—coverage for pre-existing conditions, a mandate for everyone to be insured, and assistance for those who could not afford it through some complicated machinations and creative markets and marketing. This three-legged stool functioned well in Massachusetts, and not half bad in the United States. Millions of uninsured received insurance. The rate of increase in medical spending declined. Unfortunately, from the moment the bill passed through its first rocky months, it was attacked. And then came the flood. The political flood. The legal flood. Suit after suit after suit attempted to destroy the law or provisions in the law. The individual mandate—that individuals had to purchase insurance—continues to be challenged by the broccoli argument. Despite legal challenges, most of the law remains intact, although the penalty for not purchasing insurance is gone, and people continue to buy insurance.

Whenever this pandemic ends, premiums for health insurance will undoubtedly go up the next year; some are saying up to 40 percent.[7] Millions will have lost their jobs and, with it, their employer-based insurance—a peculiarly American tradition. This means that there will be many people losing their coverage and a large number who will be priced out of the insurance market. The big question is whether this will mean a revolution? Will consumers demand universal coverage and put so much pressure on politicians that they will respond? Will taxpayers demand quality care and cost controls? Can we have both?

I doubt it. Our health expenditures are double what other developed countries have—all with universal care. Other countries have been able to sort of control costs with universal care. The pandemic has shown that our health care system is unprepared, and our response to the threat has highlighted our collective inability to think scientifically, that is, to put science above politics like Australia and New Zealand have.[8] Even if we were to magically acknowledge the importance of science and attack the technical details of policy, we are still missing the main question.

Serious health policy discussions in the United States overlook the most fundamental and necessary question to any real substantive change. Uwe Reinhardt's question, "Should the child of a poor American family have the same chance of avoiding or being cured of a given illness as does the child of a wealthy American family?[9] Implicit in most of the discussions on health care and health insurance is that the poor child does not. The debate about health insurance coverage will never progress if this question is not answered explicitly before the technical policy discussion begins.

The hope of a better system, a just system of affordable health care where every citizen has the same access to the same quality of care, will not come about despite an object lesson in how deficient our health system really is. A system that is crippled by its inability to have an adequate supply of surgical masks and refuses to answer Reinhardt's question openly is incapable of positive change.

NOTES

1. Scott, Dylan. 2020. *Vox.com Coronavirus is exposing all of the weaknesses in the US health system.* March 16. Accessed April 7, 2020. https://www.vox.com/policy-and-politics/2020/3/16/21117366/coronavirus-covid-19-us-cases-health-care-system.

2. Reinhardt, Uwe. 2019. *Priced Out: The Economic and Ethical Costs of American Health Care.* Princeton, New Jersey: Princeton University Press.

3. Gerard F. Anderson, Uwe E. Reinhardt, Peter S. Hussey, and Varduhi Petrosyan. n.d. "It's the Prices Stupid." *Health Affairs* 2 2 (3): 89-105.

4. Gerard F. Anderson, Peter Hussey, and Varduhi Petrosyan. 2019. *Health Affairs It's Still The Prices, Stupid.* January. Accessed April 7, 2020. https://pnhp.org/news/its-still-the-prices-stupid/.

5. Stewart, James B. 2012. "How Broccoli Landed on Supreme Court Menu." *New York Times,* June 14: Section A page 1.

6. N.A. 2017. *Congress.gov H.R.1628 - American Health Care Act of 2017.* July 28. Accessed April 7, 2020. https://www.congress.gov/bill/115th-congress/house-bill/1628.

7. Abelson, Reed. 2020. *New York Times Coronavirus May Add Billions to U.S. Health Care Bill.* March 28. Accessed April 10, 2020. https://www.nytimes.com/2020/03/28/health/coronavirus -insurance-premium-increases.html.

8. Cave, Damien. 2020. "Vanquish the Virus? Australia and New Zealand Aim to Show the Way." *New York Times*, April 24.

⟦ ABOUT THE AUTHOR ⟧ --

WILL DELAVAN teaches Economics at Lebanon Valley College and lives in Camp Hill, Pennsylvania, with his family Rachel, Natalie, and Alex. He thanks his insightful Health Economics class students for their ideas for this chapter.

POLITICS MAKES
NO BEDFELLOWS

BY PAT LAMARCHE

UNITED STATES POLITICS, post-COVID-19, could change dramatically. The political process in a winner-take-all system like that of the world's oldest democratic republic relies on three things: ballot access, campaign outreach, and election tabulation.

Other republics—countries run by parliaments, with substantial campaign restrictions and room for power-sharing—require far less physical contact than the U.S. system of petition gathering, constituent interaction, and in-person voting.

While all three of these components likely will change, voter tabulation presents the most significant immediate challenge. On April 7, 2020, Wisconsin held a presidential primary despite the governor's decision to postpone the election until the worst of the pandemic had passed. The Wisconsin State Supreme Court forced the election to go forward. The United States Supreme Court complicated matters further by upholding a Republican Party demand that all absentee ballots be postmarked by their April 7 election day—ignoring U.S. Postal Service policy against postmarking metered mail. If no compromise is reached, election officials must discard tens of thousands of absentee ballots—the voters' rights nullified.

Many other Wisconsin voters, expecting the election would be delayed, endangered their voting franchise. These individuals did not request an absentee ballot before the required deadline. Most voters did not anticipate the Republican Party court challenge. The court upheld the challenge after the time for absentee requests had passed. The rapidly evolving COVID-19 outbreak—coupled with the Supreme Court decision against an election day delay—forced Wisconsin voters without access to absentee ballots to either skip voting altogether or put themselves and others at risk by physically appearing at a polling station.

As the 2020 election year progresses, many states—states with more time between an outbreak and election day—have either opted for expanding their absentee balloting system or postponing the date when voters must report to the polls.

Wisconsin's 2020 pandemic predicament will keep political scientists busy for decades as they argue over whether the courts should have intervened at all.

HOW VOTING WORKS

Federal elections are regulated by states on a state-by-state basis. Presidential, Senatorial, and House of Representatives elections are not conducted by the federal government. They are managed by local municipalities pursuant to state law. The states decide which candidates will appear on the ballot. They also decide who will be allowed to vote in the election as well as how the ballots will be distributed and collected.

When the founders established the federal government, printed ballots did not exist. The voting franchise extended only to property-owning men. There is a legend that the nation's first president, George Washington, ran unopposed—but that is only how it appears. If someone voted for a different person—someone other than Washington—no record of that vote exists. Only the majority decision was transferred to the electors of the electoral college. History failed to record dissent if any existed.

In Washington's day, there was no recorded tally of the popular vote. There may have been other individuals put forward to serve as president. Without a printed ballot, every candidate was essentially a write-in candidate. Consequently, and all opposing ballots have been lost to time.

Another interesting fact about Washington's election—only ten states contributed to the final count. Because states must set the guidelines for federal elections, three states did not qualify to elect the president. New York did not participate because the state legislature had no provision for charging the electors with the power to vote. North Carolina and Rhode Island still had not ratified the new constitution. Essentially, these states were not part of the United States. The notion of holding a presidential election and not counting citizen's votes simply because a state's government had not done her legislative homework seems preposterous. But that is precisely how it works in the United States.

This enormous flexibility when controlling elections is why states hold elections so differently. Five states (Washington, Oregon, Colorado, Utah, and Hawaii) determine their winners via mail-in ballots. In two states (Maine and Vermont), everyone can vote. In three states (Iowa, Kentucky, and Virginia), felons, once convicted, may never vote again. One state (Maine) determines their contest winners with instant runoff voting—a process by which the voter states their candidate preferences. If no candidate wins a clear majority, the second choices of the lesser candidates' voters are counted. All states, the District of Columbia, and U.S. territories allow for at least some form of absentee mail-in voting. Voter enfranchisement and ballot access vary completely; most regulations fall somewhere between some far-flung extremes.

Twenty-nine states and the District of Columbia use voting machines that require the voter to touch a public computer physically. Thirty-one states require some form of a paper ballot. What will the COVID-19 pandemic do to these election processes? Will there be a national movement to make state election codes symbiotic?

In April 2020, the League of Women Voters, a universally respected voter advocacy agency, began holding webinars across the states seeking solutions to problems caused by the pandemic. Considering the pandemic, the League franchises, as well as secretaries of state across the country, endorsed some form of expanded absentee ballot system.

Maine Secretary of State Matt Dunlap oversaw a regional turnout of 73% with 35% of those votes absentee. Interviewed April 13, 2020, just hours after Maine announced the delay of their own 2020 primary, in hopes that the worst of the pandemic might pass, Dunlap explained the challenges posed when polling places are closed for safety purposes. "Expanded absentee voting is not the same as mail-in voting. Oregon and the other states mail ballots to households. Some base their mailings on voter registration, others are just mailed to addresses. Absentee ballots must be requested by the voter in advance. If Maine went to an all absentee system, we would have to start early to get the word out that ballots must be requested. I have cautioned our governor [Janet Mills] about the importance of sharing this information in a timely and efficient manner."

Richard Winger, the editor of *Ballot Access News*, sees all mail-in voting as a game-changer for states financially. States that use a mail-in system save money.

Municipalities shoulder personnel and leasing expenses. With mail-in ballots, there are no polling places to rent. Far fewer employees are required, all but eliminating additional election day payroll costs. Municipalities, working in conjunction with the United States Postal Service coordinate ballot collection. So why aren't all fifty states using this system? Two simple answers: Firstly, election results take time to compile. Americans like fast answers.

Still, thanks to social distancing, mail-in voting is coming. For 2020, additional states will expand their absentee voting. Ambitious secretaries of state may attempt a modified universal mailing. But in either case, municipalities will have to keep some polling places open for those citizens who did not have the opportunity to register absentee or did not learn about the new system in time.

By 2024, perhaps half the states will be converted to mail-in voting systems. Once the process is simplified and the financial savings become apparent, municipalities who bear the majority of the expense for elections will demand this more cost-effective system. Richard Winger thinks it just makes logical sense in light of the economic crisis that accompanied the pandemic, "We're going to have to start saving money at every level. Our economy has taken a hit. Money is going to be very important." When property taxpayers learn that they can save on elections and put that cash toward other municipal expenses, things will change quickly.

HOW BALLOTS WORK

People in the United States vote for several things on election day. Across the nation, votes may be cast for individuals seeking public office as well as fiscal bond issues. In 27 states and the District of Columbia, voters also decide legislative matters. Some states refer to this direct democracy as a *referendum* or an *initiative*. It is the method by which people vote for laws when their state legislature fails to act.

Every item on the ballot is put there one of two ways—either an officially recognized and qualified body places an item on the ballot (Major parties name their candidates—legislatures put referenda questions out for a public vote), or petition signatures are gathered to place a person or law before the people.

In the face of a deadly pandemic, the outdated practice of petition signature gathering must stop. Few republics, other than the United States, cling to this relic. Most have all but eliminated petition gathering for would-be elected officials. Georgia requires candidates who are neither Democrats nor Republicans to gather 7500 signatures to secure ballot access. Canada demands only 100 signatures to run for the House of Commons—regardless of the political party. The United Kingdom only 10.

Across the U.S., the number of signatures required varies—like everything else involving elections—on a state by state basis. Georgia's requirements are mild. In North Carolina, a new candidate—unaffiliated with either of the two ruling parties—must gather more than 80,000 signatures to run for office. With social distancing regulations and asymptomatic carriers of COVID-19 posing a health risk to the community, this sort of signature gathering rises above the level of absurdity.

One of two things will happen as a result of the threat posed by the 21st century's first pandemic. Either direct democracy will fade away or person to person petition gathering will.

Many jurisdictions across the United States allow for online voter registration. The same can be done for signature gathering. To preserve individual participation in the electoral selection process—not how Americans vote but who and what they choose between when voting—a secure online petition gathering process must be developed.

The use of the internet allows for expansion of the selection process, as well. Voter choice is too restricted in the United States. As the voting franchise was extended to more and more persons in the country, the choice offered on the ballot became more tightly controlled. George Washington may have had as many opponents as names scribbled on pieces of paper, but it did not matter because the elite establishment gave permission to vote. George Washington had the election in the bag because only wealthy men—most of whom were known to him—could vote.

Time wore on, and the population and rights of the nation grew. Once amended, the constitution allowed for women and people of color to vote, demographically changing the voter and potentially changing the race and social status of who stood for and won office. That is when ballot access became vital to the ruling elites. When anyone could vote—the powerful shifted their influence and controlled whose name appeared on the ballot.

Abraham Lincoln became president as head of the six-year-old Republican party—relegating the Whigs to the dustbin of history. Then legislatures across the nation passed laws restricting ballot access to particular party affiliations. The United States has not had a new political party take power since then.

The COVID-19 pandemic could break the traditional, closely guarded, ballot access system if new technology brings the same sort of demand for public choice to the electorate that online retailers have provided shoppers, over the past few years.

Opening the electoral process to online participation may emancipate more citizens than any other social force since Lincoln and the election of 1860. Or it could codify business as usual. Either way, the pandemic will be the catalyst for electronic ballot access.

HOW CAMPAIGNING WORKS

Social distancing has all but destroyed electioneering as we know it. Both modern-day candidates, Donald Trump and Bernie Sanders, played enormously well to packed rooms of adoring supporters. The comradery, the sense of community their campaigns inspired, allowed for like-minded individuals to see countless other versions of themselves energized for some—or all—of the same reasons. The cult of personality combined with candidate charisma catapulted both these men to the front of the political world stage.

In 2016, in the case of Bernie Sanders—a man little known outside his home state of Vermont—the rallies collected thousands of supporters together and drew the media attention necessary to become a viable candidate.

For the president—who continued holding campaign rallies throughout his presidency—these mass meetings helped him further his agenda.

By mid-March 2020, large public gatherings were all but outlawed. Groups of more than ten persons risked spreading COVID-19 and increasing the overall death toll.

Sanders—whose excitement and ability to communicate was more infectious than any virus—lost his prime method of communication when social distancing became the norm.

When individual governors started shutting the country down, few thought the distancing measures would last more than a few weeks. President Trump initially voiced hope that the nation would be back to dining out, movie-going, concert halls, and churches and synagogues by mid-April, in time to celebrate both Christian and Jewish springtime holidays.

March dragged on, and all hope for a speedy end to social distancing evaporated as the number of U.S. dead eclipsed the official number of any other nation. Dinner parties and meet the candidate events in restaurants and libraries went away when the restaurants and libraries shuttered their doors. Large and small group political gatherings—including protests—will not return in time to influence the 2020 presidential elections.

Sequestering the electorate in their homes, in front of their television and computer screens, delivers voters to all those candidates who can afford to run media campaigns. Races from school board to president will be decided by broadcast airtime purchases and anything catchy enough to spread virally along the internet.

Conventional, traditional 20th-century campaign rallies are historic relics so long as the American lockdown continues. Americans order food online. Americans visit family online. Americans read to grandchildren online. Increasingly Americans purchase everything from shoes to dogfood and wait for it to arrive at the door. Like the random packages on America's doorsteps, Americans will cease to collect information firsthand. Secondhand information will be tainted by the agenda of those who create it.

For at least a year and depending on whether a vaccine is created, U.S. voters will select candidates that translate well over the airwaves. Candidates with long resumes or lots of prior name recognition will fare better than those without the pedigree or financial resources to invent one. Voters will learn less from family and friends around them because—for the foreseeable future—there will not be anyone around. Voting will become more individual, more antiseptic, with less peer-supported thinking. Candidates will have to learn to speak one on one, electronically, to their constituents. Campaigns must help people remember their candidates from before the pandemic if they wish to prevail.

⟦ SOURCES ⟧

ACLU, Felony Disenfranchisement Laws, https://www.aclu.org/issues/voting-rights/voter-restoration/felony-disenfranchisement-laws-map.

Atlantic, The Most Important 2020 States Already Have Vote by Mail, Ronald Brownstein, April 11, 2020, https://www.theatlantic.com/politics/archive/2020/04/voting-mail-2020-race-between-biden-and-trump/609799/.

Ballot Access News, Richard Winger, April 13, 2020, http://ballot-access.org.

Ballotpedia, Ballot Access, https://ballotpedia.org/Ballot_access.

Ballotpedia, Voting Methods and equipment by state, https://ballotpedia.org/Voting_methods_and_equipment_by_state.

Baltimore Sun, Maryland's June 2 Primary will be conducted by mail with limited in-person voting, governor orders, Emily Opilo, April 10, 2020, https://www.baltimoresun.com/politics/elections/bs-md-pol-primary-hogan-decision-20200410-rvphpqz4mjfqdpnfrhjrifyqxm-story.htmlCOVID-19.

Bustle, Why Does Washington State Vote by Mail Only? The Election Allows Residents to Cast Their Ballot in Different Ways, Zoe Fergusen, October 21, 2016, https://www.bustle.com/articles/190693-why-does-washington-state-vote-by-mail-only-the-election-allows-residents-to-cast-their-ballot.

Cornell Law School, Legal Information Institute, 47 U.S. Code 606. War Powers of President, https://www.law.cornell.edu/uscode/text/47/606.

Elections Daily, Ask Elections Babe: Can elections be canceled, Genya Coulter, January 8, 2020, https://elections-daily.com/2020/01/08/ask-election-babe-can-elections-be-canceled/.

Fair Vote, The Worst Ballot Access Laws in the United States, January 13, 2015, https://www.fairvote.org/the-worst-ballot-access-laws-in-the-united-states.

Federal Voting Assistance Program, Post-Election Voting Survey 2016, https://www.fvap .gov/uploads/FVAP/Reports/PEVS_ADM_TechReport_Final.pdf.

Mount Vernon, 10 Facts About President Washington's Election, https://www .mountvernon.org/george-washington/the-first-president/election/10-facts-about -washingtons-election/.

Nerdist, Funko Announces First-Ever Virtual Convention, Eric Diaz, March 10, 2020, https://nerdist.com/article/funko-announces-virtual-convention/.

New York Times, Wisconsin Set to Vote on Tuesday After Court Overrules Governor's Postponement, Nick Corasaniti, Reid J. Epstein and Lisa Lerer, April 6, 2020, https://www.nytimes.com/2020/04/06/us/politics/wisconsin-primary-election -postponed-coronavirus.html.

NPR, Why are U.S. elections so much longer than other countries? Danielle Kurtzelben, October 21, 2015, https://www.npr.org/sections/itsallpolitics/2015/10 /21/450238156/canadas-11-week-campaign-reminds-us-that-american-elections-are -much-longer.

USA.gov, Absentee and Early Voting, Comicbook, Funko Reveals ECCC Virtual Comic-Con Details, Matthew Aguilar, March 12, 2020, https://comicbook.com /comics/2020/03/11/funko-eccc-virtual-comic-con-details/.

Vote.org, Absentee Ballot Rules, https://www.vote.org/absentee-voting-rules/.

Vox, Thousands of Wisconsin ballots could be thrown out because they don't have a postmark, Ian Millhiser, April 10, 2020, https://www.vox.com/2020/4/11/21217546 /wisconsin-ballots-postmark-supreme-court-rnc-dnc.

⟦ ABOUT THE AUTHOR ⟧ --

Award winning broadcaster, Journalist and author, **PAT LAMARCHE** stepped from behind the microphone to campaign for Governor in 1998. LaMarche translated her election success into ballot access, becoming the first and only woman to launch a political party in Maine. LaMarche was the Green candidate for U.S. Vice President in 2004.

EFFECTS ON HIGHER EDUCATION

BY VIRGINIA BRACKETT, PH. D.

U. S. PUBLIC HIGHER education undoubtedly will be reshaped by the force known as COVID-19. Once a beacon for the country, education's light has diminished due to limited access, thanks mainly to skyrocketing tuition costs and lack of public support. An ensuing competition among already weakened institutions for student enrollments has further crippled a once vigorous system. Now, the additional effects of the pandemic will be devastating. If higher education is to not only survive but thrive, the transformation of such limiting competition into cooperation may prove crucial.

To understand the long slide into decay experienced by higher education rendering it particularly vulnerable to a force like COVID-19, a brief history is helpful. The summary that follows, while hardly comprehensive, will supply that background. It also affords context for understanding the need for the metamorphosis of our educational system into a reliable, dependable model complementary to changing national values.

Traditional funding for public higher education began with the passage of the Morrill Land-Grant Colleges Acts (1862 and 1867). Privately funded universities dedicated to producing knowledge had existed for decades. But where such upper-tier private schools were intended to foster leadership skills and produce professionals, policymakers, and legislators, public schools were to focus on teaching agriculture and industrial arts.

A need for higher education in rural areas helped fuel the rapid development of land grant schools with names identifying their location, such as Kansas State University. "Flagship" state schools, such as the University of Kansas, often served urban areas. States then developed systems, placing schools in multiple cities, i.e., the University of Illinois in Springfield, in Chicago, and Urbana-Champaign. Also, two-year schools designed to teach trades not resulting in a degree, or to offer transferable classes for the first two-years in degree programs, served a local community that supported them through county taxes. Eventually, more students were urged to earn four-year degrees within any of the blossoming public college systems. Four-year schools developed different tiers to accommodate student needs and resources, with mid-tier institutions lowering entrance standards along with, some would argue, the quality of education as compared to that offered by upper-tier colleges. As the American dream of an education for all grew, so did student enrollment in public institutions, quadrupling from 3.6 million in the mid-1960s to peak in the early 2000s at about 12 million students. By the 21st century, the University of California system boasted eleven universities, while the California State University System contained twenty-three—thirty-four universities in one state alone! Competition for funding and students among public schools increased rapidly, and that was not a problem. Until it was.

By 2008, an economic recession brought to light a grim reality, the rapid decrease in public funding. Research grants and per-student appropriations dropped precipitously, and tuition spiked, culminating in a burden to students. While in 2000, tuition income outdistanced state support in three states, by 2012, that number increased to 24 states; per-student government appropriations fell by 23% and more. During the same period, tuition at four-year public schools grew by 27% (all figures account for inflation). Concurrent with a post-recession decrease in wages and an increase in poverty, the number of low-income students enrolling at universities grew, straining federal grant support. Before the 1970s, the cost of a public university degree increased at a rate less than that of inflation, but from that decade through 2013, records show an increase more than three times that of inflation: 1900 percent for four-year schools and 1600 percent for two-year schools. Presently, the most potent detrimental effect on college enrollment is likely the dwindling of a middle class that never recovered from the recession.

Some view a higher education administrative "bubble" as a significant reason for institutional debt. Others see the *U.S. News and World Report* ranking of universities that began in 1985 as a culprit. The ranking became an incentive for schools to increase spending, for instance, on merit-based scholarships, improving an institution's academic profile and its rankings. In the competition for students within a system that grew too large for the number of students needing its services, institutions offered costly incentives for students, such as high-tech libraries, hotel-worthy dorm rooms, and other "shiny objects." Reduced degree requirements helped to attract students who seemed to grow increasingly academically brittle, more prone to drop out. The system was ripe for change, such as cooperation among various universities, or takeover by an outside force. The collaboration was not forthcoming, but that external force, in the guise of business, had already stepped in.

Before the 2020 pandemic, business practices, adopted as models, helped commodify higher education. Students were re-labeled clients, institutions engaged in broader marketing attempts, and the process of earning a degree more closely resembled a shopping experience, during which customers fill their carts and check out as soon as possible. Completing an education for the sake of learning became a luxury, and academic departments were required to characterize what they could offer students in terms of future salaries. The adoption of a business model for education was not particularly successful, like trying to force the proverbial square peg into a round hole. But colleges had already invited businesses onto their campuses in the form of fast-food restaurants and chain bookstores. At the same time, payroll, human resources, and maintenance services, among others, were contracted outside the institution. Private businesses also stepped into the funding gap to support and claim the benefits of university research. In its early iteration, the research university was designed to benefit its community through the dissemination of knowledge. But with more and more of the fruits of research immediately going under patent, the "common good" was reduced to little more than an aphorism.

Business specifically became a change agent for higher education with the introduction of business-related academic majors. Historically, languages, art and architecture, mathematics, science, history, and philosophy were classic majors. But over time, newly formed credentialing majors in areas such as education and business produced degrees that offered a less-rigorous blend of ideas from each of those classical topics. And business has become adept, through advertising, at the development of narratives, a skill which educational institutions long ignored. Business knows how to develop and exploit narratives to create a need for products by connecting them to fundamental value, such as freedom of choice. So why wouldn't higher education throw in with business to guarantee its existence? COVID-19 may force that issue, by allowing through emergency actions a glimpse of what could be permanent solutions.

Partnerships already in place, such as personnel training agreements with medical institutions, can be parlayed into shared expenses and risks. Future students may simply enroll with the institutions where they hope to one day work, those businesses creating training and educational campuses of their own, with a shared network of online course delivery. That could happen as early as high school, where many students already complete online courses. And businesses could span the digital divide prompted by technology, presently available only to those who live in a Wi-Fi zone with appropriate resources. Big business can build that bridge and, ironically, support a fair economic distribution that higher education could not.

Business also appreciates micro-credentialing, a process by which workers are rewarded for training in a specific business methodology. Thus, in the business world, a certificate in a particular area carries a higher value than the more general degree. However, it also limits mobility on the part of employees who may become "lifers" locked into their training institution. While business should not become a cradle-to-grave overseer, it may offer a cooperative solution for strapped institutions of higher ed.

How might higher education avoid self-imposed obsolescence and a big-business takeover? Educational institutions could finally drop competitive attitudes and view other institutions with an eye toward survival. Recognition of weaknesses could lead to four-year institutions joining forces. That could be in terms of the ability for one campus to utilize resources of another in terms of offering popular majors, sharing faculty, and sharing administrative structure. Or a smaller school might specialize in specific majors to feed graduate programs at larger schools. Shared resources such as a statewide financial aid office or single registrar to serve all state schools would also pare costs. And some change in traditional attitudes toward education delivery and student behavior may be required.

The widespread emergency adoption of online information delivery offers a sound example. Where once online course delivery was considered less effective in educating than face-to-face interaction and a matter of choice, institutions that can't provide a sound online option for course delivery now may not be able to survive. Going forward, one super-star faculty member could offer online courses at multiple institutions with graduate students or staff shouldering grunt work, such as testing and evaluation of student assignments. A sad prediction is that as students adapt to a COVID-19 forced online learning style, part-time enrollment will likely increase for big brand colleges, helping them thrive, while erasing the mid-level college enrollment opportunities.

Another change may occur in a reassessment of the value of pre-enrollment testing, a timely and expensive aspect of preparation for college enrollment and student evaluation. During the COVID-19 stay-at-home experience, tests cannot be administered, and many institutions will likely opt not to reschedule SAT or ACT testing but will still register students. A forward-looking institution can develop a pilot program in the best lab available, its own virtual or real campus, and perhaps eliminate the need and expense of such evaluation to predict student success. Another change in student behavior may be later enrollment, with more students taking a "gap year" to assess their interests, possibly leading to better use of educational experiences. The traditional four-year degree program could collapse to three, with twelve-month enrollments eliminating the idea of a summer break from classes.

Finally, if students achieve success inside the virtual classroom, brick-and-mortar class attendance and residential sites will suffer. Should parents remain under- or unemployed, more students may elect to attend a budget-friendly community college for the first two years, few of which are residential, permanently diminishing the on-campus experience. The freshman residential year is traditionally viewed as a radical influence on a teen's transition to adulthood. That transition will look different without such socialization and preparation for real-world experiences beyond merely learning a trade. Society may also see a change in the popularity of specific academic majors, which happened following the crisis of 9/11. Studies in criminal justice, forensic sciences, and other security-related majors increased in reaction to the terrorist attacks. What shifts in focus might follow COVID-19? More scientist researchers? One possibility could be a shift *away* from what we now know as "essential" majors, such as nursing. Medical occupations will now be viewed among the most dangerous—with the least public financial support—for personnel and their families.

While not a complete solution to all higher ed's woes, partnerships with business or among higher education institutions can better deal with change by offering more flexible options. These strengthening measures may be viewed as the loss of the individualism that campuses value. However, if sharing leads to financial fitness, the sacrifice of independence may be necessary.

While we cannot know the long-term cultural effects prompted by COVID-19, we *do* know that necessity can be a mother in more ways than one. Hopefully, that necessity will be used to transform higher education beneficially. Eighteen years from now, COVID-19 young adults will be searching for their life's calling. Hopefully, a re-envisioned higher education system will play a role.

⟦ SOURCES ⟧

Blumenstyk, Goldie. *American Higher Education in Crisis?: What Everyone Needs to Know*. Oxford: Oxford University Press. 2014. eBook Academic Collection (EBSCOhost).

Theatlantic.com "American Higher Education Hits a Dangerous Milestone." Accessed April 3, 2020. https://www.theatlantic.com/politics/archive/2018/.

Insidehighered.com. "State Support Higher Ed Grows 16 Percent." Accessed April 1, 2020. https://www.insidehighered.com/news/2018/.

Texas A&M Today. "The Morrill Act Explained." July 1, 2018. Accessed April 2, 2020. https://today.tamu.edu/2018/07/01/the-morrill-act-explained/.

⟦ ABOUT THE AUTHOR ⟧ --

VIRGINIA BRACKETT, PhD, holds degrees in business, medical technology, and English. She has published 15 books and dozens of articles and stories. Her 2019 memoir *In the Company of Patriots* tells the story of her father's military service, death in Korea, and its effect on her family.

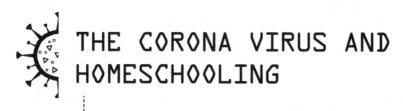

THE CORONA VIRUS AND HOMESCHOOLING

BY CHERYL WOODRUFF-BROOKS, MBA/MA

I THOUGHT OF touching on this subject because as the result of the COVID-19 virus, a vast majority of citizens in America are homeschooling. While many may be enjoying the quality family time that is lacking in homes, due to the need for a two-parent income or other circumstances, some may be pulling their hair out to keep the kids entertained and educated. Alongside cooking, disinfecting, and caring for loved ones, working from home is another part of this complexity. Maybe after hearing a taste of the history of public education, you may look at homeschooling differently.

Homeschooling is ancient in society. Homeschooling has been the norm in human society for nearly a thousand years. In America, homeschooling was directed by our first colonists. The role belonged to the mother and wife of the home who usually taught and incorporated bible study into the curriculum. The Puritans came up with the idea of public education to ensure that every household bolstered **core values** and the teachings of their Calvinist religious system. Calvinist theology covers Primitive Baptist or Reformed Baptist Churches, Presbyterian Churches, Reformed Churches, The United Church of Christ, and The Protestant Reformed Churches. With families developing their curricula, it is challenging to know for certain what, if any specific educational strategy existed in the 1600s and 1700s. The exception was wealthy families who employed tutors.

The first public education system was a college prep school for boys. The first free public school in America opened its doors on April 23, 1635, in Boston,

Massachusetts. It was an all-boys school called Boston Latin School, paid for with tax dollars. The intention was to prepare boys for college. The focus was on learning Latin, Greek, and the Humanities. Roughly a decade later, in 1647, The General Court of Massachusetts Bay Colony decreed that every town with at least fifty children should have an elementary school. Early settlers provided an elite education to males that would position them to be America's first educated leaders.

Intellectual Discrimination. In 1779, after the American Revolution, Thomas Jefferson proposed a two-tier educational system referred to as the "Laboring and the Learned." His primary concern was to advance the academic platform of those individuals demonstrating high aptitude while making no effort to supplement students who did not. The children lacking in intelligence would be encouraged to become laborers. During that timeframe, the country needed people with farming skills more than any other trade. He also suggested using tax dollars to finance this educational venture. Property taxes have been a major resource for local government in America since the 17th century and the use of this form of taxation has been prevalent since. The ideal of remedial education was absent in our culture, which was acceptable since then the need for laborers was vital to the prosperity of our country. The concern was to pluck the bright citizens out of the masses and advance their education.

Public Schools served the poor, non-religious citizens, groomed for factory work. The 1800s brought about a shift in the industries most prevalent in America. In 1805, The New York Public School Society created the vision of the classroom. They implemented the Lancasterian Model, including 100 students in one room. The significance of the classroom was *obedience* and *discipline* which was believed to be the best way to produce effective factory workers. At this time, New York had 141 teachers for a population of 75,770. Most of these teachers worked for private schools, while others taught in the charity schools run by churches, the African Free School, or the school for girls established in 1802 by the Association of Women Friends for the Relief of the Poor. About one hundred children attended the Roman Catholic school, eighty-six the Trinity Church school, and seventy a school run by the Dutch Reformed Church. Though these schools were open to all children, each religious group believed it essential to inculcate all children with religious values as well as with a knowledge of reading, writing, and arithmetic.

A Unified Public Education System began to take shape. Around 1830, most Southern states outlawed teaching slaves to read or attend school. At great risk, five percent of the African American population became literate. Fueled by waves of immigration, the manufacturing industry grew, and education took center stage as politicians and other public officials became reformers of the education system. They wanted to involve the community in shaping the needs of how free schools would operate. Two significant reformers were Henry Barnard and Horace Mann. In 1849, the Massachusetts Supreme Court ruled that segregated schools were allowed under the Constitution of Massachusetts (Roberts v. City of Boston). Segregation began in its de jure form in the Southern United States with the passage of Jim Crow laws in the late 19th century. In 1852, the state of Massachusetts passed the first compulsory school law, and by 1918, everyone had to attend an Elementary School. Blacks did not attend predominately white schools in large numbers until the 1960s.

Homeschooling became illegal in the 1970s. Mississippi was one of the first states to institute fines to parents who did not register their children for school. The changes in America's views by conservatives and liberals evolved after the Vietnam War prompted citizens, leaders, educators and reformers to dissect our education system again. Author of *Homeschool: An American History*, Milton Gaither, stated:

Given this pan-ideological commitment to local, authentic, private life and contempt for establishment liberalism, it is not surprising that members of both the countercultural right and the countercultural left reacted, for different reasons, against the twentieth-century expansion of public education into a near-universal experience.

Education reformer, John Holt took up the plight to resurrect homeschooling after it became unlawful in the 1970s. Holt, an educational theorist and supporter of school reform, argued that formal schools became repetitive and habitual. He felt that the system was designed to produce cooperative workers headed nowhere but into mediocre employment roles. Most affected by the system was the urban areas. As a result, most homeschooled children today are African American, who felt more than any other race their children were not receiving adequate education to prepare them for the future.

Is Homeschooling the better choice for a new generation? To some degree, the American public education inhibits free-thinking which could lead to ideas and invention which could benefit our country and the world in ways that must be explored. It appears that throughout most of our American history, we have steered public education in ways that benefit the needs of modern industry, without leaving much room for creativity. There are stories in third world countries when out of necessity young children have combined imagination, art, and play with their scientific knowledge to solve real-world problems. If we allow children the breathing space to develop possibilities unthought of, we may find that we have only scratched the surface of human inventions. We underuse our brain because quite possibly we have not been instructed to exercise it to a greater capacity.

Today, we have created technology that permits us to present homeschooling in a way that was never possible before and is proving to be effective. It also leaves room to infuse other skills that are quickly omitted when there is a funding deficit such as music and art. Music and art have a vital place in the growth of our children's minds. Moreover, it supplements their STEM skills. The humanities and liberal art skills can be included as well. Lastly, socializing can be tailored to suit needs and extra-curricular activities still have their place.

The decline in core values along with numerous distractions is crippling our education system. I have worked as an educator and we now have an environment that has cell phones, behavioral issues, special needs, etc. The teacher is expected to educate children with layers of other issues that need isolated attention. Not isolated children. And can we eliminate or reduce the need for taxes with kids being homeschooled? I am sure there are quite a few parents across America feeling the stress of having their kids to homeschool during this crisis. But there is an educational crisis going on in many of the free public schools. We removed religion, morals and core values from the classroom. They need to return both at home and in the classroom.

⟦ SOURCES ⟧

Historical Timeline of Public Education in the US *1647 The General Court of the Massachusetts Bay Colony decrees that every town of fifty families should have an...* www.raceforward.org.

https://fee.org/articles/the-rise-of-homeschooling-was-broad-and-bipartisan/.

https://www.encyclopedia.com/history/news-wires-white-papers-and-books/new-york-free-school-society-1805.

https://responsiblehomeschooling.org/homeschooling-101/a-brief-history-of-homeschooling/.

https://www.jstor.org/stable/30185059?seq=1.

Stephanie Watson "How Public Schools Work" 13 February 2008. HowStuffWorks.com. https://people.howstuffworks.com/public-schools.htm, 18 March 2020.

Walker, B. (1984). The Local Property Tax for Public Schools: Some Historical Perspectives. *Journal of Education Finance, 9*(3), 265–288. Retrieved March 19, 2020, from www.jstor.org/stable/40703424.

⟦ ABOUT THE AUTHOR ⟧

CHERYL WOODRUFF-BROOKS, MBA/MA is Chief Creative Officer Of Nilaja Publications. Founder of Glow Book Expo, Author, Speaker, Educator, Singer, Screenplay Writer, Marketer. Author of *Chicken Bone Beach: A Pictorial History of the Established Missouri Avenue Beach* and *Golden Beauty Boss: The Story of Madame Sara Spencer Walker & the Apex Empire.*

HOW MUSEUMS AND GALLERIES WILL ADAPT TO THE CORONAVIRUS

└o BY CHERYL WOODRUFF-BROOKS, MBA/MA

AS WE REMAIN on lockdown, museums and galleries around the globe are feeling the massive impact of empty venues and lost revenue. Consequently, the Coronavirus thrust many industries into consideration of alternative platforms such as online shopping, artificial intelligence, digitization, and virtual reality to survive. Does the question now become, do these futuristic options truly satisfy the consumer's interest in cultural institutions? Immediate action has to be incorporated by museums and galleries to sustain a presence through this devastating pandemic and beyond. And until the health experts introduce a vaccination or other forms of managing the spread, altering how visitors congregate into large cultural institutions will need to be modified.

The unbiased financial losses of public venues are being felt deeply by galleries and museums. Many New York City cultural institutions and museum directors have already begun to furlough employees and cut salaries in anticipation of budget deficits. Organizations have decided to reduce the salaries of high-level officers collecting wages of six-figures annually. Some have generously opted out of receiving a paycheck entirely to assist the company in compensating employees. Richard Armstrong, director of the Guggenheim, announced an overhaul of all salaries over $80,000 based on a graduated scale, according to an article by the

New York Post. They also announced that 92 staff members would be furloughed as the organization faces a projected $10 million shortage in revenue. The Whitney Museum of American Art recently laid off 76 employees, and Whitney Director Adam Weinberg will be taking a pay reduction in his compensation package of $1,083,525 based on Whitney's most recent tax filings.

THE ONLINE EXPERIENCE IS BOOMING – THERAPEUTIC BENEFITS OF CULTURAL INSTITUTIONS

The numerous fatalities, economic disaster, and social isolation as a result of COVID-19 have left humanity in desperate need of peace, calm, and comfort. Consequently, we are beginning to see exactly why art in all of its forms is vital to our society. For those institutions now offering a means of a virtual experience for typical museum-goers, they are seeing a record-breaking spike in viewership. The creativity of utilizing social media and the internet has brought joy to many. Science museums and the like are allowing certain species to become the new tourists in empty locations, while we all watch how they interact with seeing other living creatives in action. Boredom and the need to find other distractions from the sobering news updates of a curve of coronavirus cases not flattening quickly enough has society engulfed in the internet for any means of solace.

The rise in visitation to museums and galleries online has been rapidly increasing across the globe. In recent weeks, Google Arts and Culture—which provides hundreds of virtual tours for world-leading museums—has seen a substantial rise in traffic on their website. The British Museum's online collection page has been experiencing an average of 75,000 visitors daily. Likewise, the Courtauld Gallery's virtual tour received 723 percent more visitors last week than the seven days before.

Some cultural institutions and other entities began the process of making culture more accessible through technology years before the Coronavirus graced us with its grappling stronghold. Google, for example, already offered a scope of augmented-reality, virtual-reality, and artificial intelligence functions to enjoy. Google Arts and Culture also offer a highly-rated app, including trending functionalities such as the Art Selfie, which combines portraits and pieces of art to users' selfies. The online shift of audiences includes the Swiss modern art gallery, Hauser & Wirth, whose virtual viewing rooms have received 200,000 visits over the last month. Our temporary demise is truly allowing museums and galleries to test the waters by infusing technological advances into their platform.

MUSEUMS AND THE PUBLIC TRUST

The museum field, along with many others where public gatherings are inevitable, will need to prepare before opening their doors to the public. The American Alliance of Museums has implemented guidelines to assist when COVID-19 lockdown restrictions are lifted. According to the American Alliance of Museums, the public has a great deal of trust in the information they get from museums. I feel that way as well, having worked in a museum setting. In my experience working for the Hershey Museum in Hershey, Pennsylvania, and the Archives department of the Pennsylvania House of Representatives, I felt as though honesty and integrity of data or material collected were of the utmost importance. History is "as is." Nothing should be done to color it or implement creativity when it comes to findings. The only truth is what you have found. It is to be presented to the public as such. Hopefully, the confidence consumers have in museums will prompt them to reconvene once it is safe to get back to some normalcy. According to the American Alliance of Museums, here is why they believe the community has trusted in museums:

► Museums are considered educational by 98% of Americans, across all ages, races, and geographical locations.
► Museums are considered the most trustworthy source of information in America, rated higher than local papers, nonprofits researchers, the U.S. government, or academic researchers.
► Museums preserve and protect more than a billion objects.
► Museums are considered a more reliable source of historical information than books, teachers, or even personal accounts by relatives.

EMBRACING NEW TECHNOLOGIES - DIGITAL STRATEGY

Museums were already beginning the process of bringing archived material into the 21st century. Digitization projects have been implemented across the country. Digital strategy has been a topic of discussion for the last decade, consisting of books and conferences which included experts in the field at the highest level. Today, there are quite a few digital museums in existence, leading the way to a future that we know for sure will be drenched with technologies that surpass our current comprehension.

A book that captured my attention is *The Digital Future of Museums: Conversations and Provocations* (Winesmith and Anderson) which states that museums today can neither ignore the importance of digital technologies when engaging their communities nor fail to address the broader social, economic and cultural changes that shape their digital offerings.

Through moderated dialogue with respected and influential museum practitioners, thinkers, and experts in related fields, this book explores the role of digital technology in contemporary museum practice within Europe, the U.S., Australia, and Asia. It discusses useful ways that museums can prepare for the museums of the future, and methods that can be exercised today in anticipation of changes that will ultimately evolve in the museum sector.

Can new technologies satisfy the consumer in the same way as visiting cultural institutions?

Pandemics or not, museums and galleries have to get ready for change. Personally, my love for museums and galleries is built around the physical. The visual appeal is my attraction to them. I want to walk inside a spectacular building filled with objects that are centuries old but preserved with the utmost care. I yearn to get as close as I possibly can to a piece of artwork or object so that I can view every brushstroke and blemish on the surface. I need my senses involved in the experience beyond a computer or app. Maybe virtual reality will be enough for humans of the future because they may be left with no other choice. I can't imagine not loving the up close and personal experience of embracing life experiences in the way I do now. However, I know that we are a dynamic planet adapting and evolving with time. The only way to sustain a viable presence in an ever-changing universe is to be flexible and willing to adjust.

[SOURCES]

Cieko, Brenden, "4 Ways Museums Can Successfully Leverage Digital Content and Channels during Coronavirus (COVID-19)." https://www.aam-us.org/2020/03/25/4-ways-museums-can-successfully-leverage-digital-content-and-channels-during-coronavirus-covid-19/ March 25, 2020.

Shehadi, Sebastian. "How Coronavirus is making Virtual Galleries Go Viral." https://www.newstatemen.com/culture/art-design/2020/03/virtual-galleries-art-museums-tour-online. March 23, 2020.

Tsui, Enid, "How the coronavirus pandemic has forced art fairs and galleries online." https://www.scmp.com/magazines/post-magazine/arts-music/article/3077028/how-coronavirus-pandemic-has-forced-art-fair. March 26, 2020.

Vincent, Isabel. "NYC Museums Heads Unveil Coronavirus-Related Cuts to Multi-Million Dollar Salaries." https://nypost.com/2020/04/11/nyc-museum-heads-taking-pay-cuts-amid-coronavirus-crisis/ April 11, 2020.

Winesmith, Keir and Anderson, Suse. *The Digital Future of Museums. Conversations and Provocations*, 1st Edition. March 3, 2020.

⟦ ABOUT THE AUTHOR ⟧

CHERYL WOODRUFF-BROOKS, MBA/MA is Chief Creative Officer Of Nilaja Publications. Founder of Glow Book Expo, Author, Speaker, Educator, Singer, Screenplay Writer, Marketer. Author of *Chicken Bone Beach: A Pictorial History of the Established Missouri Avenue Beach* and *Golden Beauty Boss: The Story of Madame Sara Spencer Walker & the Apex Empire.*

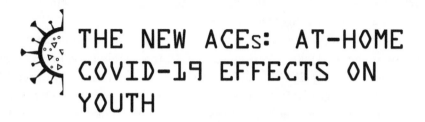

THE NEW ACEs: AT-HOME COVID-19 EFFECTS ON YOUTH

o BY WYNNE KINDER, M. ED.

TIMES LIKE THESE can challenge us to reflect on our assumptions, and on what we think we know. Here is one—many children hope for snow days, for summer to arrive, and for it to last longer than it does. They wish for more and longer breaks from school. As an elementary teacher, back in the day, I loved our first days back after a break or weekend. We would happily drift away from the lesson and into sidebars detailing the fun and adventurous things the chatty kids did while not in school. But there were gaps in who shared. There were the silent few, who I know now, were wounded by others' joy, by their privilege.

It was the privilege of comfort, connection, opportunity, and safety at home they must have envied. For some students, going to the movies, roller skating, and eating out were beyond their grasp, even their wildest dreams. Instead, they went home and wished for siblings to not mess with them in their sleep. They would hope for more blankets in the winter, for the electricity to be turned back on, and for food in the house to last past when Power Packs donations ran out. Being allowed to go outside to play was not a given. Once I knew more about their personal experiences, I stopped asking or enabling reports from anyone regarding their time away from school. Morning meetings became present-moment aware-ness practices, tasting healthy snacks, and brainstorming predictions of what we might do together in our classroom.

COVID-19 has created endless new challenges across society, within communities, and more pointedly, inside homes where children are now sequestered. Their experiences now will have a profound and lasting impact on them. For some, this period will be generally positive, for others neutral, and for the more vulnerable (whose weekends are already a nightmare), this spring is traumatic and will shape the rest of their lives with devasting results.

What kind of impact? Research on early exposure to hardship became more mainstream in the late 1990s. The original ACE (Adverse Childhood Experiences) study by Anda & Felitti (1998) found a correlation between early (up to age 18) exposure to trauma and later manifestation of disease, as well as other risk factors. ACEs include abuse, neglect, and dysfunction in the home—with a total of 10 indicators within those three themes. And since then, additional factors have emerged to keep up with the times like social isolation, rejection from peers, community violence, bullying, and poverty.

Being that the original ACEs focused on children's exposure to home-based trauma, these forced Stay-at-Home orders will severely impact many more children. Of course, outcomes will differ broadly based on multiple variables including but not limited to: family situation, degree of stability, access to resources, ability to feel safe, the temperament and mental condition of caregivers, the reactivity of the stress response among family members, as well as the protective, inner resources one brought into this pandemic.

Optimism bubbles up in social media like this anonymous, somewhat viral post:

> What if this generation of homebound youth emerges as *advanced* rather than having *fallen behind* (due to a loss of as many as 2 to 3 months of schooling)?
>
> What if they develop more empathy? Maybe even increased creativity, patience with siblings, gratitude for the simple things and quiet moments, and even a renewed affinity for reading and writing as the preferred form of connecting with others?
>
> What if they become skilled in doing their laundry, making food for the family, waving at and offering help to neighbors, organizing their own spaces, stretching a dollar, and budgeting their time?"

My heart gravitated toward such hopeful possibilities when I first envisioned them, but my heart and my experience know better. Yes, glimmers of the bright side of this global crisis exist, I honor those. Ideally, what if the new ACEs could be Advanced Coping Effects? That would be amazing—but in my community, where I teach, many children, teens, and families are (and were already) profoundly struggling.

Educators, school staff, mental health professionals, and community groups are reaching out to families in their homes. Some are successfully connecting and providing aid in comprehensive ways, while others can now assume that many families have slipped into isolation, whether intentionally or not. Thus, many children who dreaded weekends and holidays because food, caring, and safety were scarce at home, are now locked in with increasingly stressed adults. And as this period of isolation drags on and intensifies, so does their agony and trauma. Lost will be any gains made since the fall in their social connections, emotional skills, academic confidence, and sense of curiosity.

Survival takes precedence, as it should, and the most impressionable brains and nervous systems will cease to grow as they otherwise could. Wounding and regressing are sadly going to become the new normal.

As helping professionals, we must feel empowered and resourced to:

▶ continue what works and diversify the ways we reach out and support children and families in their quarantined homes,
▶ prepare ourselves personally and professionally to receive them when we return to school in the fall,
▶ put strategies in place to equip all of us to skillfully engage and nurture the most wounded and fragile among them, and
▶ ensure that we are strong, energized, and ready to connect and support each other, our students, and their families in new, trauma-informed ways.

The 2020 batch of ACEs will evolve during and after children's exposure to *new* aspects of trauma in the home and beyond to ACEs (At-home COVID Effects). What we do now and in the future will directly shape how our society rights itself after this long capsize of COVID-19.

〖 ABOUT THE AUTHOR 〗

WYNNE's 30 years of teaching includes 15 years focused on mindfulness and trauma-informed strategies through her program *Wellness Works in Schools.* She has authored classroom curricula, *GoNoodle's* mindful channels, *The Re-Set Process: Trauma-Informed Behavior Strategies* with Dyane Carrere, *CALM - Mindfulness for Kids* and graduate courses for Eastern Mennonite University.

CORONAVIRUS, INSTRUMENT OF CHANGE: HOW THE ARTS WILL USHER IN A NEW ERA

BY MARIANNE BICKETT, MA

WHEN I LOOK at photographs of my family on a trip to Lake Tahoe last summer, a quiet voice within me whispers: that was *before*. The pandemic has shaken us to our core and requires us to rethink the way we live. For example, the world feels strangely silent since Coronavirus arrived. With fewer airplanes, cars, and people out, our world is quieter; and, our air quality has improved. The present crisis is an excellent time to reconsider our transportation system. We need to face the dilemmas of our planet in addition to the immediate threat of the pandemic and plan for our future. Some changes are understandably enforced out of necessity.

Lasting changes, as I discovered as a teacher, need to begin with connections, with emotional engagement, and with expression. The arts will play a vital role in our evolution and broadening of our consciousness as we move forward. Although there is, of course, intellect involved in creating art, our vision would be far from complete without tending to our emotional truths. "It is only with the heart that one can see rightly. . . ." Saint-Exupéry's words in *The Little Prince* compliment the statement of Jacques Yves-Cousteau: "We protect what we love. . . ."[1] The arts are the language of the heart, and I believe it is through the soul's expression of our grief and of our experiences that we can journey towards healing our world. There is a new focus on large and small home gardens. I see this as a sign that we can save what we love. The Coronavirus has been the impetus of needed changes. Our emotions have stirred us to create in new ways.

As my husband and I take our daily walks around the blocks of our urban neighborhood, we have been delighted with the plethora of chalk art that families have created together, brightening up sidewalks and driveways. When the shelter-in-place order first went into effect, there were many poems featured in newspapers. I find it intriguing that one of the first things people *needed* to do was to turn to the arts. Musicians are creating ways to bring into light the angst and triumphs we face as one world. We were amused during our first week of isolation to view a video of an older couple who changed the words of a popular song into Coronavirus safety instructions. Artists and non-artists alike are finding ways to express the sadness (and sometimes giving us comic relief) of something that seemed unimaginable *before*. Our hearts have been broken open by the pandemic, and it is to the arts we look to heal. In the past, new creative expressions and innovation often arrived at the heels of catastrophe.

The Black Plague, for example, set the stage for the rise of the Renaissance. Europe's economy boomed because survivors could demand higher wages and a better standard of living. Due to the lack of laborers, technological advances followed, including Gutenberg's printing press. Scientific methods were employed in treating and preventing diseases. From that, a new era of observation flowed into the arts. Linear perspective, proportional studies, and an emphasis on naturalism indeed laid the ground for rebirth.

Following each World War, there was a boom of inventions that were a response to the wars. Useful items such as sanitary napkins and tissues, tea bags, wristwatches, zippers, stainless steel, and a communication system for pilots sprung out of World War I alone. Where there are innovations, the arts are pushing the boundaries of our imaginations. The haunting, surreal paintings by Paul Nash in response to both world wars is one example of how visual imagery changed the way people viewed the landscape of British countrysides. Aaron Copeland's *Fanfare for the Common Man*, written in 1942, was a tribute to the people who were fighting in World War II.[2] To this day, this piece yet stirs my heart in an unspoken language of dignity amid tragedy. That tragedy forces us to look deep within ourselves to find our strength and inspiration.

It is the arts from bygone eras that tell the stories that need to be heard. The Vietnam War gave us the Hippie movement, anti-war folk songs, and the uniquely American version of Pop Art. We can peer back into that time and get a glimpse of the shift of awareness by the art and music we see and hear.

Music changed our world in the 1960s by getting our attention and increasing our knowledge of situations that needed to change. I know this first-hand because I lived as a teenager through the decade of flower children and protests. Who can forget Peter, Paul, and Mary singing "Blowin' in the Wind," or Country Joe McDonald's "I Feel Like I'm Fixin' to Die Rag" ("One, two, three, four, what are we fighting for?"). Later, in 1970, Neil Young wrote the song "Ohio" after the Kent State massacre.[3] The examples are numerous, but the point is clear. Music and all art forms can be a catalyst for change by seeping into the inner reaches of our being with emotional truths.

Joni Mitchell's words in her song released in 1970, "Big Yellow Taxi"—"You don't know what you've got 'til it's gone"—were poignant then and are so again in the case of the current pandemic.[4] The Coronavirus has us cherishing our ephemeral lives. When something catastrophic happens, like a war, earthquake, fire, or epidemic, it often results in our going from fear to love. New heroes and heroines fill our newspapers. These devastating events can bring out the worst and best in us. I'd like to think, overall, with the arts to motivate us, and it is the best that wins out in the end.

In the aftermath of the Coronavirus, I see the arts expressing the images, writing the verses, and singing the songs of an awakened world. In a world where we are changed, like it or not. We cannot go back to *before*. Ever. Our books, fiction and nonfiction, and poetry will reveal inner and outer struggles as we faced the reality of a pandemic. We will come to terms with the fact that we do have an impact on our planet, and this is expressed in a renewed fervor to address environmental crises through the arts. The arts can bring us together, not to let the Coronavirus define us, rather, to empower us. We need now and will need our compositions, be they visual, aural, or in movement, to bare our truths and compel us to care and to love. To *feel* something, to want with our big, broken hearts to do something is an essential place to begin. We have confronted our mortality in a way we haven't in recent years. We now join the thousands of species in peril because of our impact on our planet. If we can reach the hearts of those responsible for deforestation through our songs and images, if we can educate those in areas where viruses have made the leap from animals to humans and help them find alternative food sources, then we can address the prevention of future pandemics. Overpopulation has brought us to this brink. Now that we grasp our interconnectedness, countries can work more closely together to solve these problems by sharing solutions and implementation of restoring habitats with education and needed resources.

It will be the arts that will act as our Universal Language. Our verses, stories, dances, music, paintings, and sculptures will serve as containers for the world's grief. Our creations will fuel a determination to reinvent the future. Music has been referred to as the language of God, for music needs no translation and can be heard and understood by everyone regardless of nationality. More than anything else, the arts can unite us. Compositions that are being conceived this very moment will touch the collective soul of the world in the near and distant future. It will force us to go to those forbidden places and question our habits and ambitions. Generations to come will look back at this time and understand, through our songs and art, the messages from a desperate time. Now is the dawning of a new age of art and inventions. Perhaps history will not have to repeat itself. Maybe the thread of our hearts pleading to be heard will carry us through challenges that lay ahead of us and keep us from making the same mistakes. Soon, I see a whole new art era emerging. As Rumi once said, "Wherever you stand, be the soul of that place."[5] That is what the arts are, our collective soul, and will be even more so as we navigate through this storm and beyond.

Although social distancing may stay with us a while, thankfully, we have music, videos, books, and art to connect us. However, the benefits of live concerts and events are essential experiences of being human, too. One of those benefits is the interaction with strangers, sitting next to someone you don't know. If we only interact with people we know, what does that do to our ability to deal with those who are different from us? Going out to someplace special, having dinner before or after, and the nuances of watching performers in person create an enriching experience that cannot be substituted. The social interactions in a museum, sharing the first glimpse of the *Mona Lisa*, for example, help us to remember better what we are viewing. I can look at a painting or sculpture in a book and be impressed, but, like seeing the *David* statue by Michelangelo in person, there is no comparison. Nothing prepares you for the real thing, to see the glow of light off the white marble, to look up and grasp the actual size of the sculpture. To experience something first hand is to see it truly.

Let us sing from our rooftops and celebrate the genius of creativity now as we shelter-in-place and in person when the time is right. Until that happy day, the arts will keep us from spiritual and emotional isolation. May our performance halls, once again, be filled with eager hearts. May our art galleries flow with the anticipation of curious onlookers. May we embrace the richness of being alive, and dance in the shadows of the Coronavirus with great enthusiasm. We will be singing new songs and creating new art that reflects our journey through this crisis. I look forward to the day when we can attend a concert again, and the immensity of the applause that will follow. The arts will draw us out of our isolation and bring us hope.

As I wrote this essay, my beloved husband, composer, and musician Brian Belét handed me something that has brought tears to my eyes. Karl Paulnack's "Welcome Address," written in 2009 for Boston Conservatory's parents and first-year students, is a validation of precisely what I am attempting to convey [6]. Dr. Paulnack's essay is even more poignant today, nearly eleven years after he wrote his speech. A pianist, he wrote about his experience after the 9/11 tragedy, how music helped people to heal, and cited stories of how music saved people who survived other horrific events like the holocaust. He wrote: "Music is a basic need of human survival. Music is one of the ways we make sense of our lives, one of the ways in which we express feelings when we have no words, a way for us to understand things with our hearts when we cannot with our minds."

The arts are vital; they are the heart and soul of humankind. Creative expressions, born out of catastrophe, will, in the end, be our salvation and keep us faithful to our intentions and dedication to the well-being of ourselves and our planet.

NOTES

1. Antoine de Saint Exupéry, *The Little Prince*, trans. Katherine Woods (New York: Harcourt, Brace & World, Inc., 1943, 1971), 87. "Homepage," Fabien Cousteau Ocean Learning Center. Online Text, accessed April 11, 2020, http://www.fabiencousteauolc.org/.

2. "Fanfare for the Common Man," Library of Congress, Washington, DC, 2002. Online Text, accessed April 11, 2020, https://www.loc.gov/item/ihas.200000006/.

3. Bob Dylan, "Blowin' in the Wind," from *The Freewheelin' Bob Dylan*, Columbia Records, 1963. Also sung by Peter, Paul, and Mary, *In the Wind*, Warner Bros., 1963. Country Joe McDonald, "I Feel Like I'm Fixin' to Die Rag," from *I-Feel-Like-I'm-Fixin'-to-Die*, Country Joe and the Fish, Vanguard, 1967. Neil Young, "Ohio," from *Ohio / Find the Cost of Freedom* single, Crosby, Stills, Nash & Young, Atlantic Records, 1970.

4. Joni Mitchell, "Big Yellow Taxi," from *Ladies of the Canyon*, Reprise Records, 1970.

5. Jalal ad-Din Muhammad Rumi, *One Song: A New Illuminated Rumi* (Philadelphia: Running Press Book Publishers, 2005), 39.

6. "Karl Paulnack's Welcoming Address," The Playground: The Simply Music Blog. Online Text, accessed April 10, 2020, https://simplymusic.com/dr-karl-paulnacks-welcoming-address-2/.

⟦ ABOUT THE AUTHOR ⟧

MARIANNE received her Master's in Art Education in 1986 from the University of Illinois. After retiring from teaching, she created *The Magic Art Cart* trilogy (2016). Marianne's next book is *Art á la Cart*, a memoir (August 2020, Sunbury Press). She is married to composer Dr. Brian Belét.

THE EFFECTS OF THE CORONAVIRUS PANDEMIC ON SPORTS

BY MERRILL SHAFFER

THROUGHOUT HISTORY, SPORTS have been an outlet for both athletes' desire and need for competition and the pursuit of excellence., and spectators' support and passion for their favorite competitors, teams, and traditions. Sports have been a means for athletes at all levels of competition to hone their skills and compete as individuals or as members of a team to seek internal satisfaction, individual and team achievement and victory, and pursue the limits of athletic ability. They have also provided the spectator with a sense of bonding with athletes and fellow fans in the pursuit of achievement, feelings of community and regional pride and the chance to witness the thrill of competition. Sports have always been a source of entertainment and a meaningful distraction from the stressors of everyday life. Whether it be a championship game at the highest professional or amateur level, a college athletic event, a scholastic competition, or a local organized or informal league, sports have become engrained into the fabric of our society. They are a source of great joy and happiness. At times of war, natural disaster and national tragedy, sports have brought our country together and provided a comforting diversion in times of great pain.

However, all of that was before we heard the words Coronavirus and COVID-19. Unfortunately, we are all too familiar with the terrible and deadly pandemic that has rapidly spread throughout the world. Daily, we witness the awful and tragic devastation that this dreaded disease has left in its wake. Hundreds of thousands of people have been sickened, and sadly, many have died at the hands of the coronavirus. Nothing can diminish the pain and suffering that have been felt by those who have contracted the virus and their loved ones. The world of sports has not been immune to the grip of coronavirus. The threat of the pandemic has brought sports, from the highest professional levels to children's intermural and beginner programs, to a sudden and screeching halt. Seasons, tournaments, leagues, games, and competitions have been postponed and canceled. For those events that have been canceled, opportunities for competition, achievements, championships, and victories have been forever lost. For those that have been postponed or delayed, the uncertainty of what is to come is unnerving and troubling. Ultimately, the virus will be controlled and contained. But what will sports (for both participants and spectators) look like post-coronavirus?

By mid-March, professional sports leagues and collegiate athletic events had been suspended or canceled. The National Basketball Association and National Hockey League suspended their regular seasons with approximately a quarter of their games and postseasons remaining to be played. Major League Soccer had suspended their season for thirty days, with a further stoppage expected to be announced. Major League Baseball canceled the remainder of spring training and indefinitely delayed Opening Day. The NCAA did the unthinkable and canceled the Men's and Women's Division I Basketball Tournaments. All collegiate spring sports were canceled. Professional golf postponed the Masters golf tournament, and The Open Championship was canceled. Professional tennis canceled Wimbledon for the first time since World War II. NASCAR indefinitely suspended its racing schedule. Japanese officials pushed back the Summer Olympics in Tokyo until 2021. All scholastic and local sports leagues and events had been canceled. The start of the National Football League and collegiate and high school football seasons are in serious jeopardy of being delayed and potentially canceled. For the first time in modern memory, the entire sports landscape has been completely shut down due to the coronavirus, with no visible end in sight.

Coronavirus has had a direct impact on athletes, coaches, executives, and media. Several NBA and MLS players, including basketball superstar Kevin Durant, have tested positive, as have an NBA coach and New York Knicks owner James Dolan. Basketball analyst Doris Burke revealed that she had also tested positive for coronavirus. New Orleans Saints Head Coach Sean Payton became the first person associated with the NFL to test positive for the virus. Although the NBA, NHL, and NCAA made agonizing choices to stop play, it appears they made wise and responsible decisions that may have prevented further spread of the deadly pandemic. In mid-February, a Champion League Soccer match was played in Milan, Italy, between host Atalanta of Bergamo and Valencia from Spain. Forty thousand soccer fans, including many traveling from Spain, flooded Bergamo for the two days. The teams shared a meal the night before the match. The event took place two days before the first reported case of community spread of COVID-19 in Italy. At least five Valencia players and a Spanish journalist were infected, and Bergamo would become an epicenter for COVID-19 in Italy, which, sadly, developed into one of the hardest-hit nations with coronavirus. Although the decisions to suspend seasons and cancel tournaments were initially viewed with skepticism and seen as overreactions, they may very well have saved lives and prevented thousands from being infected. It seems inevitable that countless thousands of athletes, staff, and spectators would have been afflicted had sporting events continued to be played during the early stages of the pandemic in the United States.

In addition to the health risks of coronavirus, there are potential effects on athletes' playing careers. With seasons and events being canceled or possibly not being finished, personal statistics and achievements are being lost. At the scholastic and collegiate levels, lost games on the athletic field may jeopardize potential scholarship offers. College athletes with professional aspirations may face lost opportunities to showcase their skills and maintain or improve their draft status. Upperclassmen at both levels face lost years of eligibility and may find their athletic careers come to an abrupt and disappointing conclusion. Olympic athletes are now faced with four years of lost training time, and older competitors may lose a final chance at world-class competition. Potential draft picks in professional sports leagues face uncertainty regarding draft status and future roster positions. At best, there will likely be abbreviated training camps and preseason opportunities for new players to learn a sport at a professional level, leaving a spot on a team roster in doubt. Current professional players not under an active contract, who are free agents, are now faced with the unknown of if or where they will play next. Aging athletes may see their professional careers come to an unexpected and unceremonious end.

The pandemic has had a devastating effect on the global economy, and sports at all levels are not immune to the economic setbacks of coronavirus. Lost revenue from canceled and delayed games and competitions has impacted sports leagues and teams, athletes, television and radio networks, advertisers, team and venue employees, and communities throughout the country. When the NBA suspended play, 259 games were remaining in the regular season, plus postseason playoff games. With the league generating approximately $8 billion per season through television contracts, merchandising, corporate sponsorships, and ticket sales, the negative economic effect of COVID-19 is staggering. Tickets sales make up nearly a quarter of the NBA's revenue. Canceled games could cost the league between $350 million and $450 million, not including the loss of postseason income. Lost merchandising and concession sales, and gameday revenue, such as parking fees, is potentially costing teams and vendors hundreds of millions of dollars in additional monies. The NBA entered into a nine-year television contract with ESPN and Turner Broadcasting worth $24 billion in 2016. The agreement pays the league an average of $2.6 billion per season. Local television contracts can provide an income of up to $100 million a year. However, clauses in these contracts can allow networks and sponsors to reduce or possibly terminate their obligations due to "extraordinary circumstances." The NBA collective bargaining agreement also has a clause that could reduce players' salaries by approximately one percent per game missed due to the coronavirus shutdown. Lost revenue could also factor into the NBA's annual salary cap, which is based on the projected income for the next season.

March Madness generates more than $800 million, approximately three-quarters of the revenue for the NCAA across all sports in a single year. With the cancellations of the men's and women's basketball tournaments, there will undoubtedly be a rippling effect on all collegiate athletics. According to a recent survey of college athletic directors, 86 percent feel that their institutions will have to make significant financial cuts to their sports programs. One-third of athletic directors projected at least a 30 percent reduction in revenue for the 2020-2021 academic year. This leads to the potential for program cuts, salary reductions, and staff layoffs.

The NHL faces similar financial issues as the NBA. Individual teams stand to lose more than $1 million per home game during the shutdown, with more significant financial losses from missed playoff games. The postponement of the Tokyo Olympics could incur a potential loss of more than $1 billion in advertising revenue. Major League Baseball ticket sales account for approximately 30 percent of the league's overall income. Lost gate revenue combined with reductions in television and radio advertising, merchandise sales and concessions, and vending income could rival the losses facing the NBA and NHL if the season is significantly delayed.

Should the pandemic extend into the fall and affect the NFL and college football seasons, the financial and social impacts could be devastating. Football is by far the most popular sport in the United States. The NFL brings in more than $15 billion in annual revenue. The league earns approximately $5 billion per season in television contracts with CBS, ESPN, Fox, and NBC. The NFL takes in another $1 billion a year in corporate sponsorships, with the remaining revenue coming from merchandising, ticket sales and concessions, and gameday income. The top 15 college football teams are valued between $400 million and $1 billion, generating hundreds of millions of dollars in television revenue, ticket receipts, merchandising, and gameday activities. Just how popular is football? During the 2019 season, 45 of the top 50 most-watched television broadcasts were NFL football games. The Super Bowl averages nearly 100 million viewers each year. College football's National Championship Game has an average viewership of more than 20 million.

The popularity of football in this country cannot be overstated. The thought of the upcoming football seasons being delayed or canceled seems unthinkable. Aside from the obvious financial implications, the impact on an already sports-deprived society is almost immeasurable. Although there have been work stoppages in the NFL in the past due to labor disputes, there was always a sense that the issues would be resolved, and the games would ultimately resume. A stoppage due to coronavirus would have a different feel and a sense of uncertainty and instability. A search of social media posts indicates that there is great fear amongst football fans that the upcoming seasons will be affected, and there is much talk of wanting the games to go on, despite the risks of coronavirus. For many, the thought of a fall without football due to the pandemic would send them into a deeper state of depression and despair.

So where do we go from here? COVID-19 will ultimately be suppressed, and sports will resume play. But when? The sporting public may have to face the harsh reality that there may be no athletic events for the remainder of 2020. If health officials are recommending that all Americans practice social distancing and that we stay in our homes for weeks and months at a time to slow the spread of the pandemic, it is truly a matter of life and death, and participating in or attending a sporting event doesn't seem to be that significant or necessary in the grand scheme. With millions being infected and thousands dying due to coronavirus and COVID-19, sports, like many other aspects of our lives, must take a back seat to health and safety. But sports will return; they just might look a little different. Players and athletes may be subjected to regular coronavirus tests to avoid the spread to teammates, competitors, and spectators. Fans and media may have to accept that there will be less player availability in the future. Locker rooms and training camps may not be as accessible as in the past, and players may not engage in customary activities, such as pre-game autograph signings or public appearances. While it is unlikely that any major league teams would fold, unfortunately, it is likely that some minor league clubs and college sports programs may not survive the pandemic. With the strain on the national economy, fans may not have the disposable income to purchase season tickets or regularly attend sporting events as they once did. Like any other business, teams may have to be more frugal and financially responsible with less revenue from advertising, product sales, and ticket income. When stadiums and venues eventually open to spectators, fans will need to be more conscious of social distancing and other safeguards to protect their health and the health of those around them.

Coronavirus and COVID-19 have certainly changed the world, and the sports landscape is no exception. As with every challenge we have faced in the past, this, too, shall pass. We will get through it together, and we all cannot wait for the call to "Play ball"!

⟦ SOURCES ⟧

Beech, John, "NFL Owner Speculates on What 2020 Preseason Could Look Like, How Coronavirus Could Change Training Camp", cbssports.com, April 1, 2020, https://www.cbssports.com/nfl/news/coronavirus-fallout-nfl-owner-speculates-on -what-2020-season-could-look-like-including-no-fans-in-attendance/Q.

Crawford, Brad, "Ranking College Football's 15 Most Valuable Programs", 247Sports, January 23, 2020.

Dodd, Dennis, "College Sports Bleak Financial Future in Wake of Coronavirus Pandemic Apparent in AD Survey," cbssports.com, April 2, 2020, https://www.cbssports.com /college-football/news/college-sports-bleak-finabcial-future-in-wake-of-coronavirus -pandemic-apparent-in-ad-survey/.

https://247sports.com/LongFormArticle/Alabama-Crimson-Tide-Texas-Longhorns -Ohio-State-Buckeyes-Michigan-college-football-most-valuable-programs-2019 -134159991/.

https://fivethirtyeight.com/features/the-coronavirus-economic-effect-could-be-staggering

https://www.chicagotribune.com/sports/ct-spt-nfl-revenue-super-bowl-20190128-story. html.

Lacques, Gabe, and Jeff Zillgitt, "How Will Sports Avoid a 'Biological Bomb' When Returning From Coronavirus Hiatus?", *USA Today*, March 27, 2020, https://www.usatoday/com/story/sports/2020/03/27/coronavirus-american-sports -leagues-ponder-how-safety-resume-games/2919534001/.

Paine, Neil, "The Coronavirus's Economic Effect on Sports Could Be Staggering," *FiveThirtyEight*, March 16, 2020.

Romano, Evan, "These Athletes and Celebrities Have Tested Positive For Coronavirus," *Men's Health*, March 31, 2020, https://www.menshealth.com/entertainment/a3144 5984/athletes-celebrities-coronavirus/.

Soshnick, Scott, and Eben Novy-Williams, "Revenue Goal Ahead of Super Bowl," *Chicago Tribune*, January 28, 2019.

⊏ ABOUT THE AUTHOR ⊐

MERRILL SHAFFER is a lifelong sports fan who grew up in Central Pennsylvania during the glory years of the Pittsburgh Steelers in the 1970s. He is the author of *A Super Steelers Journey: The 23-Year Quest to Honor Pittsburgh's Dynasty Legends*. Merrill has been interviewed on the topics of the Steelers and sports on *Good Day PA*, the *Pittsburgh Tribune-Review*, *Sports Collectors Daily*, and *The Final Score* podcast. He earned an A.A. in Business Management from Harrisburg Area Community College and a B.S. in Criminal Justice from Pennsylvania State University.

TOURISM IN THE POST-PANDEMIC WORLD

MAIA WILLIAMSON

THESE LAST SIX weeks have felt like six years. Sadly, there are so many others who also sense that the stress of this pandemic and the needed adjustments in routine, finances, and perspective have taken years off their lives. But as I type this, I am sitting in a home with electricity, heat, and a fridge stocked with food.

I am lucky right now.

Unfortunately, my young son is out of school. I can't interact with family and friends, and I've had the worst case of cabin fever. I know, so has the rest of the planet. However, the scariest part is that I'm now unemployed. As a contractual instructor at a local university, I have no job security, so I will be relying on government assistance until I get a teaching job or the benefits run out. And to rub salt in the gaping COVID wound, I teach English as a second language, which means I need international students to have a job. So, even when the dust settles, it may take a while to have enough students actually to teach.

I am *still* extremely lucky right now.

I am part of the middle class. I have a high level of education, and I come from a country with universal healthcare and a government that assists its citizens. So as inconvenienced as I am financially in the present, I will survive. I will feed my son. I will pay for my life. My profession will recover. Or I'll find a new one. I will rebound. However, I can't say the same for millions of people around the world.

Most of us don't have to look much farther than our backyards to find somebody who works in an industry that has taken a hit from this pandemic. Tourism is one such industry that has taken so many that it's hanging by a thread.

Sure, the global tourism industry periodically faces downturns. Natural disasters, wars, or financial crises may slow the tourism of a country or region and even bring it to a periodic standstill. However, we've never seen a disaster of this magnitude on such a global scale before. In a nutshell, nobody is traveling right now. And the tourism industry is dead.

◎◎◎

Millions of people around the world work in the tourism sector—restaurant and hotel workers, tour guides and operators, drivers, porters, suppliers and shop owners—who will be significantly affected by this global pause in daily life and ultimately, a means of paying for it.

As of April 14, 2020, the World Tourism Organization (UNWTO), which is the United Nations agency responsible for the promotion of responsible and sustainable tourism, projects that international tourist arrivals could decline by up to thirty percent this year. This amounts to a loss of $300 to $450 billion in global tourism exports and almost one-third of the $ 1.5 trillion that tourism generates each year globally.

The *Telegraph* (2018) notes that while most countries will feel a loss of tourism revenue to varying degrees, there are plenty that rely on tourism much more than other industries to make up a substantial portion of their GDP (the Maldives at 40%, Aruba 28% or Belize 14%). Others generate a large amount of money from tourism (Mexico at $80 billion, Thailand $36 billion, or South Africa $9 billion) to aid their already struggling economies (World Economic Forum, 2017).

To grasp how fragile the tourism industry is across much of the globe, it's essential to understand the type of economies with which we are dealing. Many countries that draw large numbers of international tourists each year are considered developing nations. They often have crippling national debt, poor government management, and limited resources for its citizens. It's no surprise then that much of the population lives below the poverty line with an impoverished health care system, poor standards of education, and few job opportunities.

However, many people without an education or marketable skills can still work in the tourism sector and make a decent living to boot. Perhaps some of these people will not draw an actual paycheck or even earn a wage but are instead reliant on the underground economy where cash is king, and tips are paramount for survival. It's these places, I argue, that we can't forget about if we want to continue visiting them.

Now I'm not debating whether we should spend money in our own countries first. That's a given. We must support our countries and cities and communities by investing in local businesses and people, and those parts of our tourism industries are no exception. Trust me; I will be the first in line to get out of the house for dinner with friends or a visit to the provincial park in my area. I also have a few trips planned in Canada, which will require me to fly. However, if international travel is your jam as it is mine, my message is not to change that when it's safe to do so.

There are plenty of places around the world where international tourism encompasses local communities in reciprocal sustainable partnerships—local communities support a tourist attraction, and that tourist attraction supports the local community.

In Uganda, I went gorilla trekking in Bwindi Forest National Park. All the rangers and guides were local. Women from the nearby villages worked at the guesthouses and lodges, cooking meals and cleaning rooms. Community members of all ages made handicrafts and worked at the local shops and family restaurants that lined the main road into the park grounds. Without the locals, the park would not run, but sadly without tourists in the park, the locals could not sustain themselves.

In Peru, I spent a week hiking the Cordillera Huayhuash mountain range in the Andes with a team of local guides, cooks, and porters. As we traversed through the mountains, we passed through many small villages where we slept and ate and were the only people from the outside who contributed to its growth.

In Borneo, I spent three days in Gunung Mulu National Park, where I did cave, kayak, and village tours with locals who lived in the communities along the Melianu River. With each visit, I made sure to purchase food or other homemade goods to give back to the communities that welcomed me. What was notable about all these places I visited, was that without the money generated from tourists, many of these communities would not even exist, let alone thrive. What was notable about all the people I encountered was that the tips I gave were far more appreciated than the meager compensation they received.

In my opinion, even when the dust settles on this pandemic and life goes back to "normal," the tourism industry will likely be one of the slowest to recover. Vacationing is probably not going to be a top priority for most of society, and when tourism does start to pick up again, it will likely be gradual. People may feel trepidation at taking trips far from home should anything go wrong, or they may forego air travel due to the expense. People may opt for travel within their own countries as opposed to going abroad to places that have inadequate medical systems and public health planning. Whatever the reason, our choices to travel will likely be measured and met with caution. And that's okay.

Nevertheless, when international travel is finally a reality for people—months or years from now—I hope we all remember some of these places that are so reliant on tourism and a cash economy. And *when* you do go, buy the crappy seashell necklace, tip your tuk-tuk driver even if it's not customary, and always try local food whether it moves on your plate or not.

If we don't give back to these communities, they may not be there when we do get around to going abroad. All that culture lost. All that history unknown. All that world left undiscovered. All those people left vulnerable. And that's the kind of world I'd rather not know.

⟦ SOURCES ⟧

"Revealed: The countries that rely most on your money," The Telegraph, accessed March 31, 2020, https://www.telegraph.co.uk/travel/maps-and-graphics/Mapped-The-countries-that-rely-most-on-your-money/.

"The Travel & Tourism Competitiveness Report 2017," World Economic Forum, accessed April 1, 2020, https://www.weforum.org/reports/the-travel-tourism-competitiveness-report-2017.

"Tourism and COVID-19," World Tourism Organization, last modified April 14, 2020, https://www.unwto.org/tourism-covid-19.

⟦ ABOUT THE AUTHOR ⟧

MAIA WILLIAMSON has been an avid traveler for over 20 years. Most of her travels have been solo and almost always with a backpack. She has been to over 40 countries and loves to climb mountains despite a crippling fear of heights. Maia writes about people, her travels, and other daily musings in her spare time (http://maiawilliamson.ca/). Her first book, a travel memoir, *Where the Tree Frogs Took Me* was published in January 2020.

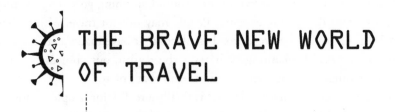

THE BRAVE NEW WORLD OF TRAVEL

BY JACK ADLER

MAY I SEE your health visa?" As a result of the Coronavirus pandemic and lingering concerns over another deadly worldwide pestilence, American international travelers soon may have to show a new document—a health visa—in addition to their passport and perhaps a regular visa for that country. Such a health visa, duly notarized by a physician, would be required as evidence that you were not likely to be the source of a virus or other infectious disease. Being subject to have a fever check is also likely before you are welcomed to conduct your business or do your sightseeing.

All governments are going to take much less for granted regarding travel as far as health goes and to do more pre-screening before borders are crossed. The public may have a short memory—though, not in this potentially lethal situation—but the travel industry will not. Each segment of the travel industry, one of the world's largest, will be forced to adapt to a new paradigm. The common theme will be more intrusive scrutiny of travelers before they board a jet, a cruise ship, or enter a country. Whether or not showing a health visa once will permit travel to all the nations part of the European Union remains to be seen.

Airlines, badly hurt by the Coronavirus pandemic, will return to "normalcy" and profits. But as passengers are confined to a crowded space, contagion can spread fast. Foodservice aloft may not improve but expect tighter controls as well as more hand sanitizers—in the lavatories. Being shown a short video on health issues, such as how to sneeze and cough, will probably be a new feature. Wearing face masks will not be an issue because by the time it became one, air travel would have plummeted. But airlines may keep a supply of masks in their expanded health kit on their jets.

Lessons will be learned with better preparations and stockpiling of needed items for quick and immediate distribution. But the mantra of social distancing will fall prey to the profit motive and sustaining the reestablishment of the travel industry to the overall economy. As the French proverb goes, the more things change, the more they stay the same. The "new normal" may prove to be an example.

Cruise ships have an even more significant problem. Even before the pandemic, these nautical behemoths carrying several thousand passengers were hurt by several instances of the less deadly norovirus spreading among the passengers and the crew. The pandemic, however, brought about ships unable to dock for a while because of stricken and dead passengers or crew members. While passengers have the run of the ship, for the most part, they are still in a limited space. Lines will doubtless tout advances in telemedicine that can be employed aboard their ships, but how much value such especially useful developments would have in an epidemic is dubious.

One of the great lures of a cruise holiday is visiting ports of call. But these ports may want more timely assurances of one kind or another on who is disembarking on their shores. A health visa presented onboarding may not suffice. Accordingly, cruise lines may give a fever test to each passenger getting off the ship, either on a tour program or independently. Of course, port officials may also conduct their own health checks.

In the same vein, cruise passengers should expect a mandatory talk by the ship's doctor on health issues. A video is also likely to be shown. Free sanitizers will probably be available in cabins.

The most significant change is likely to come in the tour business. Participants on tours are banded together most of the time. Tour guides are keenly aware of not losing a stray member of a group as they visit sightseeing attractions. Most tour takers are not necessarily seniors but still on the older side. Fears of the public in being caught in a confined situation may need to be addressed by tour operators. Sizeable discounts may be given. Any motor coach tour will find itself in the same predicament. To a lesser extent, rail travel will also call for travelers to possibly once more show their health visa, and perhaps be subject to an updated fever check. Look for less fully escorted tours, where you are always with tour members, and more semi-escorted programs where travelers can set up their itineraries to some extent. Self-drive tours are an example.

In a similar vein, independent travel may also see a rise, especially in riskier forms of travel like skydiving, spelunking, and other extreme adventure pursuits. Ironically, the embedded threat of another pandemic may influence younger travelers to decide to live it up while they can. Travel suppliers are always looking for new frontiers, and travel of one kind of another to the Arctic region will grow if not deterred by political arguments between Russia and Western governments, including the U.S. and Canada.

The diminution of tours will affect retail travel agents by reducing their revenue from this source. The commission structure by which travel agents are paid may undergo a sea change as airlines and cruise lines will be doing more themselves to counteract public concerns and as air-sea programs retract.

Hotels, also likely to expand in size and amenities, may ask to see a health visa too, and conduct a fever check while you check-in. More sanitizers will be in rooms, and hopefully, hotels will not add a tab for these items.

Overall, the industry will want to show how concerned it is about public fears. Many astute marketing minds will be at work devising ways to entice and reassure potential travelers in ads, brochures, and other promotional material. Travel insurance will also be substantially affected. Currently, coverage for epidemics is excluded from most policies on a force majeure basis. Such coverage may be increasingly offered, but probably at a stiff premium. Repatriations of remains are likely to show a hike.

Another element in what the future may portend is a significant growth of virtual travel on television, the Internet, and the development of new apps. The three-dimensional impact will be increasingly significant. Many travelers may well be satisfied by the illusion of walking on the Great Wall of China or navigating the step-pyramids and hieroglyphic stairway on the Mayan ruins at Copan in Honduras, while still in the comfort of their homes.

The appeal of travel itself, lamentably, may suffer as the threat of a pandemic— and being sick and possibly stranded somewhere far from home—becomes an unavoidable and lingering component in everyone's thoughts. Discounts may not be enough for some people to offset these concerns. But the longer life goes on normally, the higher the chance that travel will return to its rightful role.

The memory of coronavirus will not deter significant developments in the future. There will undoubtedly be more high-speed rail. Larger jets may not allow more legroom, but they will require expanded airports, which in turn will cause friction with cities. Larger cruise ships will carry even more passengers, as many as five thousand, while offering more amenities and port of call diversions.

Welcome to the brave new world of travel.

⟦ ABOUT THE AUTHOR ⟧ --

JACK ADLER is the co-author of *Travel Safety,* which the Library of Congress had translated into Braille, and *Smooth Traveling for Seniors.* He was a weekly columnist, on a freelance basis, for the *Los Angeles Times'* travel section for nearly 15 years. He also served as the Feature Editor of *Travel Weekly*, a leading industry publication.

CONSERVATION IN
THE MIDST

BY BROOK LENKER

THE EVISCERATION OF normalcy from COVID-19 may ripple through society for years. Time will tell, but even as the crisis unfolds, good seeds are germinating. Kids stroll with their parents. Eager hikers tackle trails. The virus weighs on minds, but the outdoors call. Out of the angst, hope may emerge, manifest in stronger ties between land and people, and a broader societal commitment to environmental stewardship.

With proper social distancing, nature and wellness are intertwined. A 2018 study from the University of East Anglia found spending time outside has significant and wide-ranging health benefits, that "exposure to greenspace reduces the risk of type II diabetes, cardiovascular disease, premature death, preterm birth, stress, and high blood pressure."[1] Coping with a pandemic didn't make the list, but maybe it should. Research suggests natural areas can also boost the immune system and reduce inflammation.[2]

With the curbing and cancellation of athletic events, vacations, and large gatherings, people turn to parks, trails, and forests for entertainment. Anecdotal reports abound of open spaces teeming with eager adventurers. The Appalachian Trail Conservancy has had to request federal agencies to close the national scenic trail, due to ". . . the incredible increase in usage at many of the ANST's most popular sites."[3]

Richard Louv's 2008 book, *Last Child in the Woods: Saving Our Children from Nature-Deficit Disorder* launched a national dialogue about children's lack of exposure to the natural world and the linkages "to some of the most disturbing childhood trends, such as the rises in obesity, attention disorders, and depression."[4] With parents home with children and everyone yearning for things to do, coronavirus may be the impetus to dig into backyards and green places, to discover or *rediscover*, the humble pleasure of mucking about. The wilds, even those close to home, nurture physical and emotional fitness while stoking imagination.

Studies suggest cultivating concern for nature is likely to lead to positive environmental behaviors.[5] The connection, the *grounding*, that roots from exploration expands ecological awareness. Environmental literacy grows. Conservationists blossom.

The vulnerabilities of living among contagion open minds to the fragility of the world, including the risks of existence on a warmer planet. In 2015, the Intergovernmental Panel on Climate Change found human emissions of greenhouse gases to be "the highest in history," with a clear influence on the climate system. Further impacts were expected.[6] The World Health Organization concluded, "Changes in infectious disease transmission patterns are a likely major consequence of climate change."[7] Ironically, studies suggest a linkage between the severity of coronavirus and air quality. Researchers at the Harvard University T.H. Chan School of Public Health found that "higher levels of the tiny, dangerous particles in the air known as PM 2.5 were associated with higher death rates from the disease."[8]

Coronavirus hasn't only led people outside, its decelerated life and demonstrated the virtue of basics, of getting by with less stuff, and wasting fewer hours behind the wheel. With reduced use of fossil fuels, the air clarifies. Satellite photos of Wuhan, China, under quarantine show a city with crystalline skies, unearthed from relentless smog that sickens and kills.[9]

As we slow down, walk more, and drive less, will a new frugality permeate our future decisions and practices? Will financial strain curb or reconfigure our spending priorities? Will utilitarian reinvestment in and around our homes (e.g., energy efficiency, vegetable gardens, shade trees) trump lavish expenditures? It's too soon to know, but the virus seems to weave the fabric of family tighter and hew an acumen of caring. Alterations and sacrifices in our daily living *may* change us forever.

Not everyone has the same carbon footprint or footprint on footpaths. Low-income persons already live more simply by necessity, and their access to the outdoors, to cope or connect, is limited. The pandemic disproportionately impacts impoverished communities—a symptom of crowded living, occupational hazards, inequitable healthcare, and greater exposure to poor air quality.[10] Climate change poses greater challenges to those least able to move or adapt.[11] These groups will no longer be ignored. They seek and deserve a steady dose of Mother Nature—and a healthy, sustainable future.

A small idea, sparked in April 1970, flowered into a global observance. People mobilized by the thousands to testify to the defilement of the planet *and* to demand bold action. Humanity exercised humility, a *de facto* declaration of biospheric interdependence. While the momentum of the first Earth Day event wavers year to year, the 50th occurrence—a significant milestone for ecological consciousness—is ripe opportunity to ponder stewardship shortcomings and fertilize aspirations. Awakened by dueling crises, we might travel the forsaken road towards environmental and economic justice *for all.*

Progress is painful but persistent. The case of the internal combustion automobile is instructive. Electric cars have them slated for extinction—it's only a matter of how fast. Volkswagen plans to sell 28 million all-electric vehicles by 2028 and outsell Tesla.[12] Seattle and Los Angeles have pledged to have diesel- and gas-powered cars banned from parts of their cities in about ten years.[13] Promise abounds, but plunging oil prices due to evaporating demand and oversupply may put a drain on battery-powered transport for months, even years, to come.

The free will conundrum is a knot, tough to untangle. In the same neighborhoods where roofs sprout solar panels pushing clean electrons, the pavement is marked for more fracked, natural gas hookups, extending the clean fuel myth and dangerous reliance on climate-killing fossil fuels. Maybe COVID memories of bluer heavens will kindle desires to propagate them, permanently

Breaking out of in-home lockdown, the woods beckon. *Terra Firma* feels alien underfoot. Spring explodes in cordial colors. Songbirds frenzy at feeders. Garter snakes ascend into sunshine. Trees bud and bloom. The creek performs a soundtrack for the jubilant scenes—contrary to the misery that shrouds a season of despair. The elixir of beauty peels lethargy away. The bounty liberates and inspires. Will it be heeded without being reaped?

Walt Whitman knew, ". . . the secret of making the best persons, it is to grow in the open air and to eat and sleep with the earth."[14] Humans mystify, but hope abides. We're all poets ready to write the future. Our time has arrived.

NOTES

1. "It's Official—Spending Time Outside Is Good for You." ScienceDaily. ScienceDaily, July 6, 2018. https://www.sciencedaily.com/releases/2018/07/180706102842.htm.

2. "It's Official—Spending Time Outside Is Good for You." ScienceDaily. ScienceDaily, July 6, 2018. https://www.sciencedaily.com/releases/2018/07/180706102842.htm.

3. "Baxter State Park Will Delay Opening to a Target Date of July 1 Due to COVID-19." The Trek, April 15, 2020. https://thetrek.co/appalachian-trail/appalachian-trail-conservancy-urges-thru-hikers-postpone-hikes/.

4. Richard Louv. "Last Child in the Woods - Overview - Richard Louv." Richard Louv Blog Full Posts Atom 10. Richard Louv. Accessed April 15, 2020. http://richardlouv.com/books/last-child/.

5. Parfitt, Joshua. "What's the Best Way to Inspire Positive Environmental Behavior?" Pacific Standard, March 16, 2018. https://psmag.com/environment/inspiring-environmentally-conscious-

6. The Core Writing Team, Rajendra K. Pachauri, and Leo Meyer, eds. 2015. "IPCC Climate Change 2014 Synthesis Report." *Intergovernmental Panel on Climate Change.*

7. "Climate Change and Human Health - Risks and Responses. Summary." World Health Organization. World Health Organization, October 25, 2012. https://www.who.int/globalchange/summary/en/index5.html.

8. Friedman, Lisa. "New Research Links Air Pollution to Higher Coronavirus Death Rates." The New York Times. The New York Times, April 7, 2020. https://www.nytimes.com/2020/04/07/climate/air-pollution-coronavirus-covid.html.

9. "Airborne Nitrogen Dioxide Plummets Over China." NASA. NASA. Accessed April 15, 2020. https://earthobservatory.nasa.gov/images/146362/airborne-nitrogen-dioxide-plummets-over-china.

10. McGreal, Chris. "The Inequality Virus: How the Pandemic Hit America's Poorest." The Guardian. Guardian News and Media, April 9, 2020. https://www.theguardian.com/world/2020/apr/09/america-inequality-laid-bare-coronavirus.

11. "Report: Inequalities Exacerbate Climate Impacts on Poor." United Nations. United Nations. Accessed April 15, 2020. https://www.un.org/sustainabledevelopment/blog/2016/10/report-inequalities-exacerbate-climate-impacts-on-poor/.

12. Loveday, Eric. "How Volkswagen Plans to Sell More Electric Cars Than Tesla." InsideEVs. InsideEVs, March 12, 2020. https://insideevs.com/news/403865/vw-outsell-tesla-electric-cars/.

13. Kershner, Ellen. "Will Gas Cars Eventually Be Illegal in America?" WorldAtlas. https://www.worldatlas.com/articles/will-gas-cars-eventually-be-illegal-in-america.html (accessed April 15, 2020).

14. Whitman, Walt. "LEAVES OF GRASS." The Project Gutenberg eBook of Leaves of Grass, by Walt Whitman. Accessed April 15, 2020. https://www.gutenberg.org/files/1322/1322-h/1322-h.htm.

[ABOUT THE AUTHOR] --

BROOK LENKER received his bachelor's and master's degrees in Geography from Towson University. A lifelong conservationist, he directs the nonprofit FracTracker Alliance, addressing environmental and public health risks of oil and gas development. His novel, *The Restorers*, is an environmental suspense story set on the Susquehanna River.

ON THE ECONOMIC FRONT

⌐o BY SIMON LANDRY

THE RECENT OUTBREAK of COVID-19 will have impacts that will be felt for many decades to come. The two most significant impacts will be how the economy will be transformed and how the West's relationship with China will change.

On the economic front, I believe that the first transformation that will happen will be that most western countries will begin to reappropriate their production capabilities. The rise of globalization has most likely reached its peak, and we now see, during this pandemic, that we have become too reliant on foreign and emerging markets to produce goods at lower prices. There used to be a time when we could build and manufacture pretty much anything and everything we needed domestically. The rise of globalization and the constant pursuit of maximum profit for investors during the last few decades have pushed companies to ship production overseas so that they could maximize their investors' returns, but all that has come at a cost. It has created a vicious circle that is now difficult to break free of.

When a consumer chooses to buy an item, say a t-shirt, that was made in China for a lower price, instead of the slightly more expensive one made in America (where workers were adequately compensated), that consumer may have the illusion that he has made a wise economic choice, but when you repeat these buying habits on a larger scale, it forces the American company to ship its production out of the country so that it may remain competitive. Said company will have to lay off all its workers. These workers, now out of a steady income, will start buying cheaper goods made overseas themselves, forcing yet another manufacturer to shut down, creating more unemployment, and so the vicious circle continues to turn. The current pandemic now shows how vulnerable we are to these emerging economies, particularly with medical equipment shortages. When these countries face adversities like the one we are now all facing, they are not able to fabricate the goods on which we depend.

As I stated earlier, the current economic model is not sustainable on a long-term basis, and we will have to rethink our consumer habits. When an electronic company sells a new cellphone for $1000, expert analysis calculates that the phone itself costs around $300 to $400 to manufacture and ship to consumers. Such a high profit margin is indeed interesting for the company's investors as their investment return is very high, but the same item could have easily have been fabricated locally and would have cost around $800 to manufacture, all the while cutting shipping expenses. A $200 profit on a $1000 phone is still very good, and it creates local jobs and new consumers. We must remember the times where America had a vibrant economy with small towns built around a manufacturing plant. Such a transformation would indeed take some time to come to fruition, but it can be done. The only real deciding factor will be the consumer's willingness to bring about these changes, choosing to spend a little more money for items that are made locally, knowing all the positive impacts it can have on his country's economy, or choosing to continue to look for the biggest bargain possible and allowing their money to end up in another country's pockets. In the end, it is in our own hands.

The second significant change that will be brought about by this pandemic will be our political relationship with China. For too long, the world powers have turned a blind eye to China's transgressions, as we have become more and more dependant on them economically. The internment of their Muslim citizens in "reeducation camps" in northern China has been well documented. China's support of rogue regimes like North Korea is the only reason such countries can keep operating the way they do. Working conditions in many Chinese factories have been exposed over the years, like suicide-prevention nets in some electronic factories to keep employees from taking their own life at work, and is something no western nation would tolerate on their own soil, yet we turn a blind eye to it because we continue to depend on these factories to build our consumer goods at the lowest cost possible. But the Chinese government's corruption and sheer incompetence have never been as dangerous as with this recent outbreak. It has been well documented that China knew about COVID-19 way before it turned into a global problem, but they chose to attempt to cover it up, going as far as to silence health care workers who tried to sound the alarm. Unfortunately the genie was already out of the bottle. If the Chinese government had been open and transparent about the outbreak from the beginning, other nations could have quickly taken preventive measures earlier, and the outbreak could have been contained. Now, because of the way China chose to operate, the entire planet is suffering from this virus, and it will cause a global recession not seen since the Great Depression.

It will not be easy for the US to come back from the massive lay-offs and the two trillion dollars it has borrowed to face this crisis. The first step that should be taken by world governments is to erase their Chinese-held debt immediately. The US debt to China is currently around one trillion dollars. The US should forfeit that debt immediately since China is directly responsible for the two trillion-dollar budget measure that has just been taken to fight this pandemic. The other measure that the US could take the lead on is to convince the other world powers to strip China's seat on the UN's security council. This is not the first pandemic that has originated from China (swine flu, avian flu, and H1N1 have all originated from China). It is difficult to see how a country which has brought the World to its knees and caused hundreds of thousands of deaths around the globe by their incompetent management of a local epidemic can have a say about the planet's "security." The American government could take the lead on this, and other nations would surely follow.

It will take a long time for the planet to recover from this pandemic, but just like other global events that have taken place before, like World Wars, it will bring about significant changes in our society. Although most of us will not be alive to see the long-term effects of these changes, we can nonetheless get to work on transforming our society for the benefit of future generations.

⟦ ABOUT THE AUTHOR ⟧ ---

SIMON LANDRY lives in Montreal. He is a graduate of Laval University and works in education. He is the author of the thriller *Chestnut Street* and is currently working on his second thriller novel.

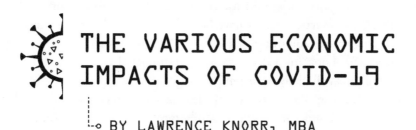

THE VARIOUS ECONOMIC IMPACTS OF COVID-19

○ BY LAWRENCE KNORR, MBA

WHERE TO BEGIN? Let us just cut to the chase. Many of the other writers in this volume are touching on the personal and specific aspects of society. This chapter provides a survey of the various potential impacts on the economy, focusing primarily in the USA. Changes that were already underway are likely going to accelerate. The shutdowns due to COVID-19 will likely cull the weakest players from the field and will potentially transform some sectors for years to come, if not permanently.

Following are the likely impacts by sector, from the largest to smallest by Gross Domestic Product (GDP):

REAL ESTATE, RENTING, LEASING (13% OF GDP)

Most people think of real estate as homeownership, but this sector spans commercial real estate as well. On the homeownership side of things, people will still need shelter, so this will only be affected insofar as buyers maintain their credit and are able to buy. There may be a shift away from some areas and to others based on where COVID-19 outbreaks occurred, but usually real estate purchases follow jobs, family, or other quality of life concerns.

In the short run, it is probably a good time to buy a house as interest rates remain low, and the inventory has been queueing during the lockdowns. As a seller, the opposite is true for a while. If you must sell quickly, you will need to market well to stand out in front of the others. If you are on no timetable, consider holding to your price and waiting out the downturn.

On the commercial end of things, it is a vastly different story. While the apartment and condominium leasing business will likely rebound, leasing to retailers and restaurants will be most affected. Also, leasing office space may have a more prolonged rebound than residential space as more businesses consider staggering work from home opportunities and use the moment to rethink their overhead decisions. Brick and mortar retailers have been fading from the scene, except for grocery and drug stores. Anything that sells on Amazon in large volumes likely has been impacted. Look for a depression in retail-related real estate. Likewise, lessors to restaurants will likely have a much longer road to recovery. It is possible that most Americans, given the temporary loss in income, concern about their health, and the newfound enjoyment of family meals at home, will reduce their visits to restaurants for years to come. This is especially true of buffets!

STATE AND LOCAL GOVERNMENT (9% OF GDP)

In areas most affected by COVID-19, where the lockdowns were most impactful to state and local economies, it is highly likely tax revenues are significantly depleted. Regions that rely more heavily on state and local governments tend to have and higher tax rates and, by coincidence, were more impacted by COVID-19. This has to do primarily with population density. While tax revenues from real estate or other property ownership are likely minimally impacted, transactional taxes on sales and use are significantly impacted, especially taxes from brick and mortar retail and restaurants. Look for tax increases in the future to cover the shortfalls as well as a reduction in services wherever possible. It is unlikely the federal government will provide every dollar needed to cover state and local deficits.

FINANCE AND INSURANCE (8% OF GDP)

Retail banks will likely consider changing how they interact with customers, adjusting more to drive-thru, ATM, and home banking capabilities and de-emphasizing the need for office visits.

Banks, in general, will review their loan portfolios and are likely to be impacted by defaults among the tens of millions of unemployed and many failing businesses. While they may be flexible in the short run with extending payments, there will be an effort to reduce risk in the long run.

Businesses going for loans in the future might be required to carry business continuity insurance or will be screened for my likely they are to be affected by future pandemics and other risks.

The investment industry has already primarily moved online and is not likely affected much from an operational perspective; however, they are affected by the renewed awareness about portfolio risk among their clients. Brushing up on risk models and reevaluating investments, post-COVID-19, will likely lead to changes in mutual fund and ETF management.

The insurance industry is likely most affected by COVID-19—especially health insurance. There is likely to be a renewed push at the national level for a better solution to health insurance. Democrats will likely push a new single-payer plan while Republicans will push a private solution. Any solution will need to be more portable and address pre-existing conditions, including those who were infected by COVID-19 and for whom we have yet to study its long-term effects.

The life insurance market is likely to change with additional questions and screening related to COVID-19 like the addition of AIDs screening decades ago. At this time, the actuaries have no idea what the long-term impacts of surviving COVID-19 are and may be reluctant to assign anything but a higher risk level.

HEALTH/SOCIAL CARE (8% OF GDP)

Outside of the insurance implications discussed already, healthcare delivery is likely to change. Telemedicine is likely to gain traction to reduce cost and wait times for a majority of otherwise healthy patients. Look for this to begin to transform the typical doctor visit. Most insurance companies will likely mandate this as a first step in any non-emergency care.

Given the trend towards telemedicine, doctor's offices and clinics will likely transform over time to be a place where only the really sick or those requiring physical procedures will be present. This will require an even higher standard of hygiene, which is likely to expected by most people going forward. Expect offices to require masks and provide hand sanitizers in the waiting rooms. Expect more cleaning in between patients. Expect an in door and out door approach to funneling patients through the process.

Regarding pharmacies, we have already seen an increase in mail-order and home delivery of medications. This will continue in tandem with telemedicine. Drugstores who do not adjust to this trend will likely find their traffic and margins declining.

DURABLE MANUFACTURING (6% OF GDP)

Durable goods are things that tend to last for years. Think cars, appliances, guns, tractors, etc. If you are an automobile manufacture, you have likely had no one in your showrooms for many weeks. New car inventories are likely much higher than expected. We had a booming economy before this hit, so production levels of most durable goods were high. If you are in the market for a new car or truck, you will likely see some of the best deals in your lifetime over the coming months—low interest rates and lots of rebates. The downside is the used car market. If you have a vehicle to trade, you will likely be offered less as the buyers focus on the new car deals for a while.

The same will be true for purchasing just about anything durable. Look for deals for newly manufactured items but difficulty selling used.

RETAIL TRADE (6% OF GDP)

This was already discussed to some degree in the real estate section. Retail has been gradually shifting from brick and mortar to e-commerce for many years. This bout with COVID-19 is likely to kill off the weakest of retailers, while it has strengthened those most engaged online. Neiman Marcus announced a bankruptcy recently at the same time Amazon was registering record sales.

The exception to this has been grocery stores. They have seen a near doubling of their business as people buy nearly all their food at the store as opposed to dining out. This sudden shift has led to supply chain issues despite an abundance of available food. Products that were packaged for the restaurant and service industry and not for consumers are now held up and may be wasted.

Those retailers that remain can take lessons from the grocers who thrived during the outbreak. They quickly innovated the use of PPE and implemented better hygiene practices. Some also adjusted the flow of traffic in their stores and better accommodated online ordering, delivery, and curbside pickup practices. All these things are likely to remain to some degree and may be necessary for survival.

Restaurants were virtually out of business nearly everywhere for weeks. Those that remained in business were able to process online, takeout, or pickup orders. Given the likelihood of changes to restaurant layouts and seating plans, it will be necessary to maintain a vigorous takeout business going forward.

WHOLESALE TRADE (6% OF GDP)

When you think of wholesale, these are the middlemen who sell to the retailers and manufacturers. Many are manufacturers themselves. At the root of this is the transportation and logistics industry that moves goods across our nation. These players did a remarkable job so far during the epidemic. Wholesalers who sold to restaurants and institutions likely saw a big downturn. However, those that serviced the e-commerce players and the grocery and drugstores likely were remarkably busy. This section of the economy will continue to do well but will adapt to the shift in priorities among the various channels.

NON-DURABLE MANUFACTURING (6% OF GDP)

The sudden shift from a booming economy to a depression has immediately impacted the buying habits of most consumers. The demand for luxury and higher-end goods likely declined significantly, while the demand for basic consumer staples, especially food and PPE, skyrocketed. While the economy is frozen, this will continue. When things begin to open, and the unemployment rate begins to recede, we will see a recovery in the luxury goods.

However, it must be said the primary concern in this area, outside of food, is that we manufacture so little in this country. We are dependent on imports from China and other countries. We make very few shoes and almost no apparel in this country. A lot of our medicine is mixed elsewhere. Most of our PPE is made overseas. The list goes on and on.

This is one area where national security is paramount, and the government will be further regulating and providing incentives for the on-shoring or near-shoring of more industries that produce consumer staples, at least to a safety-stock level.

FEDERAL GOVERNMENT (5% OF GDP)

The national government just added more debt in one year than at any time in our history. The long-term trend will be a need to increase taxes and decrease payouts. Rational leadership in Washington, D.C., would take a closer look at expenditures and go about further reducing the cost of government. It is highly likely recent tax cuts will be rolled back. It is also likely the government will be part of an international effort to get China to pay for its missteps. This could go so far as some debt cancellation or other reparations but will not be an easy road.

Given the amount of money created out of thin air to finance our various bailouts and handouts, one would think our currency would devalue, and inflation would take hold. We have the least sick of the major currencies and are experiencing a strong dollar. This helps us through this predicament, providing a cushion and privilege that no other nation has. However, as we come back out of this, especially if we come back strong, we could experience inflation and devaluation. In the meantime, we are fending off the deadly death spiral of deflation.

INFORMATION (4% OF GDP)

Big data and artificial intelligence will be the wave of the future. The transition to more online sales and activities requires more analysis to understand customer wants and desires and to market to them in a more targeted and effective way. The information sector was mostly unaffected by the COVID-19 outbreak. Many employees engaged in this activity remained at work, working from home as many of them do at least part of their time. Expect this sector to continue to do well. Its employees could lead us out of this depression through their continued consumption and spending on discounted durable goods.

ARTS, ENTERTAINMENT (4% OF GDP)

Events that happen in arenas, stadiums, theaters, and other venues have been canceled or postponed. The idea of packing 50,000 or more patrons into a small space is utterly contrary to the health guidelines we have been provided. It will be interesting to see how long until this business recovers. How soon will these stadiums fill up again? Will they ever?

To counter this doubt, online and broadcast events will continue to well and maybe even better if the fans stay home in their living rooms. The movie industry is an excellent example of this. More and more, we see films skip the theaters altogether and show up for download on our entertainment services. How many movie theaters will survive the pandemic? Will patrons think to see a show on the big screen worth the risk?

The many ancillary businesses affected by this are the various vendors who service these events—everything from food and drink to security. These organizations are likely to cut back for some time.

Do not expect a comeback at the arenas and stadiums until we have all been vaccinated.

CONSTRUCTION (4% OF GDP)

Believe it or not, many states shut down construction businesses during the lockdowns. This was probably unnecessary for those activities that occurred outdoors and with social distancing as a standard practice. Construction crews are rarely in close quarters, and many wear masks or other PPE as part of their routines.

That said, in the long run, it will be interesting to see which construction projects continue and which do not. There will probably be little impact on housing construction but a negative impact on commercial retail construction. Think of the myriad of properties that were already emptying and will now be bereft of tenants. These former retail spaces will need to be torn down or refitted and repurposed—another sideline in this sector.

If the governments fund an infrastructure package of some kind, we could see many public construction projects such as roads, bridges, and airports. This would provide a boom to the local economies but may not have the long-range impacts desired if fewer people fly or drive out of habit.

WASTE SERVICES (3% OF GDP)

Waste disposal is a big business in our consumer culture. The recent uptick in consumer purchases (groceries) instead of dining out has likely shifted to an increase in consumer packaging waste and recyclables. There was already a glut of recyclables in the marketplace. Where to go with all the plastic and paper?

Waste disposal is with us for the near and long term. These industries may need to change some practices related to hygiene but should otherwise be unaffected.

OTHER SERVICES (3% OF GDP)

No, we are not just talking about certain services in Las Vegas here. This could be just about anything from tattoo parlors, to hair salons, to office cleaners. There are so many small businesses in this sector, too. Those that quickly adapt to the PPE, hygiene, and social distancing guidelines will do well. Those that do not will see a longer curve to recovery. They may even see their demise if customer habits change out of fear. Services that primarily work outdoors, like landscapers, painters, gardeners, etc., will see little impact on their businesses. Services that must enter the home or office might have new requirements to implement.

UTILITIES (2% OF GDP)

Electricity, gas, water, sewer, etc., are all essential basic services that will continue to be so going forward. The only concern in these industries is about managing dunning processes and monitoring for risk from specific sectors.

MINING (2% OF GDP)

When we think of mining, we usually think of coal miners in Pennsylvania or West Virginia, or gold miners in California or Nevada. This sector also includes oil extraction, which is a big business in the USA. At the time of the pandemic, the USA was the largest producer of oil and gas in the world, relying heavily on shale deposits that must be fracked. The price to produce a barrel of crude oil in the USA is much higher than the oil produced in the Middle East or Russia.

Given the nosedive in demand for transportation fuels, there was a supply glut in the marketplace that soon became overloaded due to the lack of storage capacity. This, coupled with a price war perfectly timed by Russia and Saudi Arabia, caused oil futures in the spring of 2020 to reach negative levels for the first time in history. This meant the producers could not give the product away. They had to pay someone to take it away.

To the producers in the USA, prices below $30 for a barrel of oil is devastating. Prices in the negatives are unfathomable. Many of the weaker small players will go bankrupt in the short run. Look for consolidation in the USA and quite possibly tariffs on oil imports.

It is far cheaper to maintain our self-sufficiency in oil as opposed to paying for wars in the Middle East to protect supply chains. Look for a shift away from protecting those supply lines to increase risk in the marketplace, and therefore increasing the value of domestic production.

If you are a truck driver, airline, or automobile traveler, expect the price of gasoline to be low for a while—maybe even eighteen months or more—until the over-supply situation is alleviated.

CORPORATE MANAGEMENT (2% OF GDP)

The accountants, consultants, and lawyers will always make their money. Enough said.

EDUCATION SERVICES (1% OF GDP)

We have just seen a tremendous forced shift from brick and mortar schools to online delivery. The lessons learned from this will lead to opportunities to further exploit. Look for growth in online education tools and services, especially when it comes to distance learning management and delivery.

Parents and students will screen institutions for these capabilities if they do not do so already. One must wonder if the days of the brick and mortar college campus will soon be history.

AGRICULTURE (1% OF GDP)

The growing and raising of plants and animals for consumption will continue unabated. What is grown or raised and to which wholesaler it is sold might change. Also, the opportunities for export could change dramatically if there is a decline in relations with China.

◉◉◉

Switching to an international or global level, we must also consider the trade relationships within trade zones and between nations.

CANADA/MEXICO

Our nearest trading partners are also the largest recipients of our exports. We are also their most significant trading partners. This North American trading relationship is essential to develop further on-shore and near-shore supply chain capabilities going forward. Look for more production to shift from China to Mexico and other Central or South American locations.

CHINA

Given China's role in the spread of COVID-19 and the government's behavior during the pandemic, it is highly likely the USA and most of the rest of the world will rethink their reliance on China for manufacturing capabilities. This was already starting to happen, but the sudden disruptions in supply chains for some products highlighted this predicament. China is likely to be the big loser in this going forward, experiencing a gradual drain of their export manufacturing base. Look for China to shift towards building their consumer markets through domestic production to ward this off. The problem is this would require a loosening of the reins by the Chinese Communist Party.

EUROPE

The European Union has struggled to hold together during the COVID-19 crises as poorer southern countries like Italy and Spain suffered more than the more affluent northern countries like Germany and the Netherlands. With Brexit already underway, Europe is becoming a German-dominated entity. This will only last if the other nations are willing to adhere to strict fiscal management in Brussels. Also, they are likely to take on new trade initiatives like the USA, seeking to consolidate supply lines on the continent. The USA and Europe would do well to continue to collaborate on trans-Atlantic trade as the trans-Pacific ebbs.

UNITED KINGDOM

There is an exceptional opportunity to further cement trade relations with the post-Brexit United Kingdom. It will be interesting to see if post-COVID-19, the Brits wish to continue to distance themselves from the nearby Europeans. If that trend continues, deeper ties with the USA make sense, integrating Britain more with the vast North American market while Europe squabbles.

JAPAN/AUSTRALIA/NEW ZEALAND

As concern about China gains focus, these countries will seek to distance themselves from dependency on China and will strengthen ties with other regional players and North America.

INDIA

India could continue to gain in importance given its close historical ties to England and the prevalence of English as a second language. Information Technology services have grown over the last twenty years. Expect that trend to continue. India will also likely turn away from China and focus more on other regional players, Europe, and North America.

MIDDLE EAST

The oil industry is a mess, and the USA has become the leading producer of oil and gas, albeit at a higher price. The crash in prices hurts these export-dependent countries very deeply, so a return to sustainable price levels is likely to occur at some point. However, expect the USA to pull back from protecting these regimes as their strategic importance diminishes.

SOUTH AMERICA / SOUTHEAST ASIA / AFRICA

The rest of the world is not among our largest trading partners. However, there has been an increase in imports from Vietnam, which seems to be the country of choice for shifting some production out of China. This could be a first hop in redefining and diversifying supply chains. Look for other trading opportunities to develop as the world begins to rethink how it supplies its needs.

◉◉◉

In the days of Adam Smith and *The Wealth of Nations*, the concept of absolute advantage regarding trade was defined. China seems to be the nation in recent years in this driver's seat. David Ricardo further augmented this model with the concept of comparative advantage, meaning nations would trade relative to what they can do productively. In other words, while China might be the least-cost producer, there is enough of a market for others who are relatively effective in doing so for a portion of the market. There is another model in the works that recalibrates based on risk and not just cost. In other words, when you consider the total potential cost of a trading relationship, the real cost of exchanging goods is beyond just the price of labor and materials. It also includes the value of disruption, the loss of jobs and infrastructure, the negative impacts on local economies, and the health and well-being of the populace. When all these costs are considered, a real comparative advantage will value proximity and security more highly. COVID-19 has taught us this lesson in spades.

⟦ SOURCES ⟧

Sawe, B., 2020. The Biggest Industries In The United States. [online] WorldAtlas. Available at: <https://www.worldatlas.com/articles/which-are-the-biggest-industries-in-the-united-states.html> [Accessed 27 April 2020].

Workman, D., 2020. America's Top Trading Partners. [online] World's Top Exports. Available at: <http://www.worldstopexports.com/americas-top-import-partners/> [Accessed 27 April 2020].

⟦ ABOUT THE AUTHOR ⟧

LAWRENCE KNORR, MBA, has been teaching business and economics at the college level for nearly twenty years. He has also worked in executive roles in information technology, is the founder and CEO of Sunbury Press, Inc., and is the author or co-author of over twenty books.

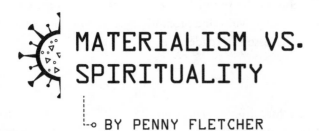

MATERIALISM VS. SPIRITUALITY

○ BY PENNY FLETCHER

ENGLISH ROCK STAR John Lennon's famous song "Imagine" came to mind immediately when I thought about what could come of this worldwide crisis called Coronavirus—imagining a world at peace without hatred or fear; of people helping to eliminate homelessness and hunger; caring for each other no matter what their race, religion or stature on the economic scale is truly a beautiful vision.

Forced to stay inside for an extended period—much more time than most of us would have chosen—many may contemplate life in ways they never have before. Perhaps they will learn to meditate, or they will pray with a new or renewed sincerity. And maybe, just maybe, what is discovered will be how mysteriously and quietly inter-related we all are. Like all the great Masters: Jesus, Buddha, Mohammed—and others—have shown us, the plight of one is the plight of all. Perhaps racial, religious, and cultural barriers will fade, and we will realize we are all members of one race: The human race, and no matter how we worship or what our creed, creation and thankfulness for it belong to all of us.

That is what I mean when I refer to spirituality. We can see it in the smallest things. Like the other day when I watched a young woman I know does not have anything to spare, take sandwiches and coffee to a man holding a sign, "Out of Work."

In Tampa Bay, where I live, the homeless are always present. The poorest and most vulnerable in our country tend to migrate to warm climates and stay in groups in the woods, usually behind stores and restaurants they know regularly get rid of outdated or unused food. Since COVID-19 came to town, Tampa's Metropolitan Ministries is sheltering almost two hundred families, including more than three hundred children, while continuing to dispense hot meals and bags of food, week in and week out, to people in lines of cars and on foot. Volunteers there say they always have a crowd, but since COVID-19 came, they are stretched beyond anything they have ever seen before. The volunteers are tired, but that does not mean they will quit.

Although much of the media tends to focus on negativity, stories of selflessness and heroism have come through more lately, courtesy of COVID-19. A few weeks ago, I saw a news story on television about a seventy-two-year-old Italian priest, Don Giuseppe Beradelli, who gave up his ventilator to a child, and later died. This followed my reading a feature about Maine landlord Nathan Nichols who allowed all the renters in his two-hundred-unit apartment building to forgo paying rent in April. More spirituality.

And every day, faces of unnamed doctors and nurses in hospital corridors and emergency rooms cause me to be thankful that many fellow inhabitants in a world (that too-often shows favor toward those of wealth and power) are thanking those who carry on their daily functions behind the scenes. That many are seeing, and are grateful for, their sanitation workers, grocery clerks, and others working in masks and gloves to assure our communities continue to provide us the basics.

It is especially good to know that most of the world's religions are continuing to provide hope and strength using FaceTime and Zoom and other methods that have been made available on computers and phones. These technological wonders were not invented at the time of the 1918 Spanish Flu epidemic. People back then were not told regularly about the latest safety measures, and worse, unless they lived in the same town, they were not able to connect with those they loved as we can today.

Perhaps there will be more people in the churches, synagogues, temples, and mosques when COVID-19 leaves. It is evident in many places online that prayer for each other is at an all-time high. Will that translate to a more loving and communal living style when the virus leaves? A daily lifestyle where people care for neighbors they never knew before? Maybe even to more spirituality and less rigidity toward another person's worship practice?

We are taught that early civilizations lived in tribes; each person assigned tasks to help the whole. The way the world is blacktopped and built upon now makes it so fast-paced it is hard to slow things down to a speed that allows us to stop, get away, and be in the moment. For that is all we have, this one moment. Everything else is either in the past or future, and those are not in our immediate control. So, what shall we decide to do with this moment, this "now"? I know several people who are reading books they have not had time to read before. Others who are learning new modalities or health routines and even languages they always wanted to explore.

I have a job that allows me to work from home, so my life has not been as disrupted as most. But my heart breaks for the thousands of families who do not have that luxury. When studies show that as many as eighty percent of Americans live paycheck-to-paycheck, and we know that number was higher in many other countries *before* COVID-19, it makes some wonder exactly how much we need in our lives. I have had this discussion with friends, both before and during this outbreak. One of them said it would be good if those without necessities could barter; maybe, offer services for necessities instead of relying on money.

Will this time without paychecks lead to more thoughtfulness about our spending patterns? If we are living close to the edge, do we *need* a third or fourth pair of shoes? A new coat or piece of furniture before we put more cash away?

It is almost funny how, when the parks and beaches are closed; suddenly more people realize how beautiful nature is. How we want to go for a walk in the sand or on soft, dewy-wet grass, and seek out the sounds of chirping birds and chattering squirrels and smell the sea? Walking downtown is not the same now either, without the smells of fresh-baked bread and cakes and pies coming from the vents of restaurants, or the sounds of children playing hide-and-seek behind post-boxes and under front steps.

So many of us want what we cannot have today. Right now, that means to go about our "normal" way of living. But wait—maybe there is more to learn so we can create a new normal—a better normal than we had before.

Is this one of the lessons COVID-19 will leave? Will we be more ready to pray for others, instead of handing out a quick, "I'll pray for you," when we hear bad news, and then forgetting about it as we go about our day? Will this mean many have used this time to further their inherent spirituality? It is inborn, encoded in our human DNA, although some may not call it spirituality. Some may think of it as merely being grateful for the Earth, sky, and sea.

When this awe, or gratitude, is forgotten or left out somewhere along the way, as humans, we can turn to "things" to make us happy—to fill the void. When the latest fashions, cars, and large homes filled with things that need dusted and cleaned become the goal of life, that is what I am calling materialism.

Yes, it is nice to have beautiful things, but having too much can be a burden too. How will I keep it? Will someone try to steal it? How many locks should I use? Maybe part of our internal void can be filled by merely handing a sandwich and coffee to a person holding a sign that says, "Out of Work," like the young woman I saw last week.

Materialistic values tell us, "If I give something away, I may not have enough," while spiritual values say, "When I give of what I have, I gain more." Maybe it does not all equate to money. Maybe we get something back as peace of mind, or better health, or a happy feeling that we made someone else's day. We can use this time to sulk over not being able to live normally, or we can create a better world by creating something new in us. It will not matter if it is a painting, or a poem; learning to meditate or writing a letter to an old friend. In the long run, everything produces after its own kind. Doing something worthwhile now will always come back to us in some way. All the great Masters said it. They just employed different languages and words.

⟦ ABOUT THE AUTHOR ⟧ --

PENNY FLETCHER is a long-time student of Metaphysics, and has watched science and spirituality come together searching for the creative spark called 'life.' An author, editor, and coach, she works on-line with authors all over the globe, and believes every Soul is created, loved, and aided by angels of God.

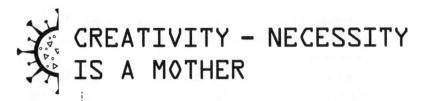

CREATIVITY - NECESSITY IS A MOTHER

BY CHRIS FENWICK

WHEN WE STARTED brainstorming about what kinds of topics should be in a book regarding the effects of the COVID-19 pandemic on society, I knew I wanted to write about creativity and how this innate quality of humankind could and would save our future. That sounds fantastic, but then, so is creativity. If humanity ever had a superpower, it's our ability to imagine and then create new solutions to existing problems.

The challenges we face as a nation and as a race are extreme. Even before the Coronavirus spread to every nation and territory around the globe, in a matter of days, we faced an uncertain future. Global climate change, poverty, nuclear weapons, and megalomaniacs with both political and firepower threatened us. But even while we struggled with what we used to think were terrible threats, a few experts saw what a deadly pandemic could do. While most of us were blissfully ignorant, maintaining business as usual, these visionaries peered ahead and began formulating responses. When we finally caught on, it was too late to stop the epidemic from spreading across the globe. Still, these visionaries—creative problem solvers and experts with specific expertise—are what we need to meet this test, as well as other challenges that lie in wait to overtake us.

Of course, humanity is familiar with adversity. Hard times tend to put life into perspective. Facing a pandemic and watching the death count climb could make you decide to live life more fully or make you shut down and hide. Finding it hard to purchase the everyday products you need, could push you to be creative in ways you never knew were possible, or it could make you feel fearful and desperate. Necessity could be a mother or *the* mother of invention. We invent in less adverse times, but need pushes us harder to use parts of our brain that sometimes lay rusty and unused.

The hardships we face now range from inconvenience for some to profound risk to health and home for others. Where we were when this all happened—financially, in our relationships, and developmentally—has a lot to do with how we are weathering this storm. For many, nothing could be worse, and survival instincts take over the brain, while creativity fights for a moment here or there. It's hard to think outside the box when you live in one on the street. Those with the least among us, are suffering the most. My heart breaks for them.

For the rest of us, our struggles range dramatically. Some can still access their creativity and look for solutions to new problems. We imagine what could be, what should be, and how to bridge the gaps between here and there.

We don't yet know the lasting impact of the Coronavirus and subsequent disruption in economic opportunities, but we can look to history and see similarities. The Great Depression, beginning in 1929, is known as the worse economic downturn in US History, lasting ten years. Other factors contributed to the longevity and severity of that depression, including the Dust Bowl that caused a shortage of food and killed many.

Now, we can also see, as "hindsight is 20/20," that American ingenuity and perseverance were alive and active at this time. What follows are six inventions that we currently use every day, each born from the Great Depression era. Each one contains a metaphor—an example of the type of ingenuity we need now. As you read, allow them to inspire and prompt you to explore new ways to use that fantastic creative mass atop of your shoulders. We need ingenious people like Colonel Schick, Malcolm Wheeler-Nicholson, and Franklin Delano Roosevelt; we need you!

A hundred years from now, our grandchildren or great-grandchildren will read articles about what came from the global pandemic known as the Coronavirus and the economic challenges it left in its wake. They will talk about their imaginative family members, who used this time to create things that are, for them, run-of-the-mill, ordinary items they take for granted. You can choose what kind of creative thinking for which you'll be remembered.

BUTTERMILK PANCAKES - RETHINKING SOUR MILK

Some people today don't know what buttermilk is, but they know they like buttermilk pancakes and biscuits. Buttermilk has been around since we've had butter as it is the liquid left over after you churn the butter out of milk. It is low in fat but contains most of the protein originally in milk. Real buttermilk ferments into a thick, tangy cream. Today most buttermilk is cultured and pasteurized, making it a bit different from what our parents or grandparents might remember during the Depression. It is sourer and tarter than sweet milk.

Farmer's have been accustomed to buttermilk and using it in recipes forever, but for many poor during the Depression, buttermilk became wildly popular. Some say it was because factories began creating cultured buttermilk, and that is true. But according to my late mother-in-law, Gracie Fenwick, buttermilk became a staple in households during the Depression instead of regular milk because it was a third the price and easier to get. If you consider that a rural family of five could get the same amount of protein in buttermilk for a third the price during the Depression, now you know why your grandparents developed a taste and found many new uses for it. It seems the sour and acid attributes of buttermilk accents pancakes, biscuits, potatoes, and other dishes perfectly, giving them a more robust and delicious taste. Who knew? Your grandparents knew.

I doubt they cared for it much at first, but like many things, when you're hungry, your taste buds have to adapt to what is available. Much of what is considered 'southern food' is comprised of ingredients (okra, collard greens, pig parts, duck liver, morels, etc.) that previously were snubbed by Anglo buyers. Tough times forced people to use them, create ways to make them palatable, and in the end, they became a part of our regular diet and menus today.

We don't need a global pandemic or depression to change our collective palette. Ramen is a staple of most college kids and can be made into the most delicious meal with a few modest ingredients and very few cents. Even small hardships cause the creative juices to flow.

So, what are we making today, that typically wasn't considered acceptable, but now is not only acceptable but even preferred? For some, we are limiting our trips to the grocery store to lessen our exposure to the disease. We try new combinations and experiment. For others, we're trying to stretch that dollar as far as possible.

It doesn't have to be just food. But I think we may see our taste buds and our everyday lives acclimate to these circumstances because we had to be creative, adaptive and are, either forced or are willing to try new things. Some creative endeavors happen while we are moving forward, albeit kicking and screaming along the way.

SPAM - REPACKAGED JUST IN TIME

Like buttermilk, Spam responded to the need of the time–a cheap, protein-rich product that had a longer shelf life. Spam is a meat product made by Hormel using less popular cuts of pork, ham, and combined with spices, cornstarch, and preservatives to create a popular, easy to transport, versatile meat. Many fresh foodies hate it. But for low-income households, it provides just what they need, when they need it—anytime—since it lasts forever.

Spam's most versatile attributes are its transportability and shelf-life. Its popularity continued and fed our troops in World War II, around the globe.

Hormel took a low demand cut of meat, combined it with a few products, created a new way of manufacturing—Spam is cooked in the can—and delivered it to fit the need of the times. Even if you don't like Spam, you can't deny Hormel's creativity for a just-in-time product to meet the needs of millions. Spam has stood the test of time too; it turns 82 this summer and may well see a comeback in popularity in tough times ahead.

THE ELECTRIC RAZOR - WINNERS DON'T QUIT

Changing pace, the electric razor, invented by Colonel Jacob Schick, has a longer story. Colonel Schick spent time in 1910 in Alaska and grew tired of lathering up in ice-cold water for his morning shave. That's when the idea of an electric razor first came to him. But his plans got side-tracked when he was recalled to active duty in World War I. During the war, he was inspired by repeating arms and imagined a replaceable razor head. After the war, Schick invented the forerunner to the replaceable blade razor, which was successful, then sold it and used the money to return to his original idea–the electric razor.

But it was now the Depression, and no one wanted to manufacture it. So, he started his own company and filed the first patent in 1930. The design was still clumsy, with the motor independent of the razor, and it didn't catch on right away. But the colonel didn't lose faith. He mortgaged his home and worked on the design, putting the motor in a sleek hand-held device. The new model went on sale in March 1931. Most would say his timing was way off. To make sales more difficult, the price tag was $25, which is about $360 in today's money. But the colonel found his market and sold 3000 in the first year. By the end of the Depression, he had sold well over 1.5 million units.

With unfortunate timing and a high price tag, to what do we contribute Schick's success? Some will cite that the cost of replaceable blades, shaving cream, and other accouterments needed for a regular shave added up in the long run, so the price tag wasn't that bad. Some will say the era of electricity and first adopters were excited by new tech and a new toy. Some will attribute his success to marketing his product to those who could afford it. All of these are probably true, but I suspect there is another not-so-secret ingredient in the colonel's success. It's obvious when you read about his life. Colonel Jacob Schick was determined and believed in his product. Nothing would stop him, not a shortage of cash, not a Great Depression, not rejections from other manufacturers–nothing. In the end, Schick retired a rich man, and the electric razor is here to stay.

There will be products that come out of this period, and we'll be amazed at how they survive and thrive. Maybe you have one of those ideas brewing in your mind. Or maybe, you have already begun the process but now are rethinking the release of your new concept to the world. Take heart. Colonel Schick would tell you not to give up, and you know what? He'd be right.

SUPERMAN - DISTRACTION AND HOPE

Before big blockbuster movies, Superman launched as a small comic book. As a matter of fact, all comics were created during the Great Depression. Malcolm Wheeler-Nicholson founded the first comic magazine called *New Fun* in the mid-1930s. The original comics didn't do well, but in 1937, Malcolm created *Detective Comics* (DC). Malcolm had to declare bankruptcy, but the company continued, and in 1938, Superman was born as the incredibly strong man who triumphed against the worst of enemies.

Early comics, went through a lot of hardships and criticism–everything from censorship to a mass outcry protesting their violence, complaining about them for distracting the youth and turning them into delinquents. Some simply said comics lacked true artistic expression.

But comics withstood the test, providing what the country needed—distraction and hope. At a time when there wasn't a lot of good news, comic books, and then radio shows based on the same stories, distracted people from the direness of their situation. They also provided hope, as everyday citizens read about or listened to the morally upstanding strongman who could save the day. Superman became the embodiment of hope for the future.

Comics have often been relegated to a subculture of young people or dismissed entirely. But that's not reality. In the year following Superman's comic book release in 1938, it sold 1.2 million copies. By the 1940s, Superman was joined by Batman, the Human Torch, the Sub-Mariner, the Flash, and Wonder Woman. Proof positive, a creative distraction and ray of hope were sorely needed by the people living during the Depression.

In today's world, we have entertainment everywhere, and we value it highly. Superman and many other comic heroes have filled the big screen and our culture. We don't need convincing of the power and need for distraction. We can access it anywhere, anytime. But I wonder what genres will come out on top in the months and years to come. What messages will the population gravitate to, and what will inspire the youth of our generation? I suspect hope will be a prominent and popular theme because when times get tough, hope is what we all need most.

NATIONAL PARKS - HELP WANTED

In 1933, President Franklin Delano Roosevelt founded the Civilian Conservation Corps (CCC) as part of the New Deal to give much-needed jobs to Americans out of work. The CCC gave men lodging, food, and pay for working on conservation projects throughout the country. The CCC is credited with planting over three billion trees across nine years—trees that reduced erosion and provided shelter from wind and drought that contributed to the Dust Bowl. The CCC was one of the New Deal's most popular programs, building miles of roads and trails, stocking rivers and lakes with fish, and fighting forest fires.

One of the reasons this program was so successful is because it gave people purpose. Sometimes, the situation is so dire; you need a handout. But over the long term, people need a hand-up, a goal, a job to do, for a decent wage. As we see unemployment hit new highs, this is the type of program we might need in the months and years to come. These initiatives could come from the private sector, but more likely, they'll come from government—state and national. I understand the sentiment of small government, but I also know there are times when we need a well-working, wide-reaching federal government. In times of war, pandemics, and national economic hardships, we need innovative, compassionate leaders at the top who can bring people together and roll out new programs to get people back to work. It might not be for parks and trees; it might be for bridges and infrastructure. Many areas need attention. These kinds of programs might be foundational for a family or a community. When you vote, remember these programs and consider who will be this creative.

THE FUTURE DEPENDS ON US

In the meantime, don't be too fast to judge others until you've walked in their shoes. If you can give a hand-out or a hand-up to someone who needs it (encouragement, creative ideas, services), this is the time. We're in this together, and the future depends on us.

The world is more complex and interconnected than during the Great Depression. Even while we are forced to stay at home—else we risk sickness or infecting others—we are more connected to more people around the world. If this type of pandemic happened even fifty years ago, the outcome would be much different. Scientists, a world away, are collaborating on tests and vaccines, treatments, and equipment. This has never been done on this scale before because we have never been here before. This interconnectedness allows us to collaborate and create in new ways, and at a whole new level. We might repurpose things that weren't seen as useful or palatable prior; we could repackage old products just in time. We all must persevere to deliver products in which we believe. We can create hopeful distractions while we step through the worst of it; and we can envision new programs to get back to work. Some of our creativity will save lives, some will give purpose, and some will provide hope. All are important.

Creativity *is* humanity's superpower. We might not be made of steel like Superman, but we have amazing brains that, when faced with extreme difficulty, can either hide away, lay down and die, or get up and be inspired to create something new. Our kids will judge how well we perform and how creative we are during this pandemic and the economic situation that follows. Buddhist monk and award-winning Korean chef, Jeong Kwan, said, "ego and creativity cannot exist together." I think what she means is that sometimes, we must get out of our own way. If we can leave the tendency toward self-importance behind, believe in our offering, and be willing to work together, we can see new levels of creativity never imagined. Necessity is the mother of invention, and we've not seen this level of need combined with this level of connection in the entire history of our species.

Sometimes, we wait for permission to be creative. Please allow this time of crisis to be all the permission you need. Often, we crave space to be imaginative. Clear a table, a desk, a room, a corner, a piece of paper, or a new document, if you must, but make the space. Some need quiet to find the creative impulse inside. Headphones might be an option or a walk alone while we are engaged in social distancing. Extroverts often require collaboration as they develop their inventive impulses. Zoom, GoToMeeting, and FaceTime are easy tools to connect with others online. If you set the agenda ahead of time, you'll be more productive. Whatever you need, find the space, time, and resources required to fire-up that pre-frontal cortex in your brain, and then stay healthy, determined, and don't give up. I look forward to seeing what we all create next. Your superpower awaits!

[SOURCES]

Ruth, K., 1983. Taste for Real Buttermilk Acquired in the Depression. [online] Available at https://oklahoman.com/article/2045618/taste-for-real-buttermilk-acquired-in-depression [Accessed 25 April 2020].

History.com Editors, 2020. Great Depression History. [online] Available at: https://www.history.com/topics/great-depression/great-depression-history [Accessed 25 April 2020].

Stidham, L., 2020. 5 Brilliant Inventions That Came Out of The Great Depression. [online] Available at: https://historycollection.co/top-5-american-inventions-come-great-depression/ [Accessed 25 April 2020].

Robins, B., 2018. Things Invented Because of The Great Depression. [online] Available at: https://www.grunge.com/133358/things-invented-because-of-the-great-depression/ [Accessed 25 April 2020].

So, J., 2013. The War Against Superman. [online] Available at: https://www.newsweek.com/2013/06/12/war-against-superman-237560.html [Accessed 25 April 2020].

Cantu, A., 2016. Into the Comic World: Superman and the American Anxieties in the Great Depression. [online] Available at: https://stmuhistorymedia.org/into-the-comic-world/ [Accessed 25 April 2020].

History.com Editors, 2018. Civilian Conservation Corps. [online] Available at: https://www.history.com/topics/great-depression/civilian-conservation-corps [Accessed 25 April 2020].

[ABOUT THE AUTHOR]

CHRIS FENWICK is a writer, technical project manager, and ecommerce professional. She has been writing, publishing, and engaged in storytelling for over a decade. Her first novel, *the 100th human* remains one of Sunbury Press' all-time bestsellers. The third and fourth book of her record-breaking fiction series, *State Changers*, releases in 2020.

CPSIA information can be obtained
at www.ICGtesting.com
Printed in the USA
BVHW032350140520
579725BV00003B/11